Advance Praise for "Tell Me the Number before Infinity"

Very powerful narrative in two voices. This book should be required reading for teachers and everyone in equity and critical disability studies. It demonstrates that the discourses of pity and denial, set in motion by other humans, may well influence how people with disabilities and their allies including parents and other loved ones live. But disabled people live with joy and pleasure along with the despair from living in social worlds so intolerant and incapable of dealing with differences. People with disabilities live lives that go beyond the narrow confines of a normalizing society. I will have it as required reading for my critical disability studies course.

—Gloria Filax, Professor of Disability Studies, Athabasca University

~

Tell Me the Number before Infinity *is enlightening, moving, often funny, sometimes enraging, and just a plain old good read... it's a big thing to feel one's life has been changed by something—and reading this book has done that for me.*

—Kathryn Chetkovich, author of *Friendly Fire*

~

This is a surprising book—unsentimental, sparse, courageous and loving. The mother's voice. The child's voice. Two remembered stories of lives impacted (but not defined) by cerebral palsy. Moments simmered down into pithy, revealing, understated segments. This is a story of a family always focused on the child's full humanity and capacity, and of the child (now an adult) trailblazing her own, unique path in the world. A must read for teachers, social workers and parents. It will change how you think about cerebral palsy and families.

—Julie Olsen Edwards, Early Childhood, Family Life Education Specialist, Cabrillo College faculty, co-author, *Anti-bias Education for Young Children and Ourselves*

~

I sat down to read a few chapters and could not put this book down. Beautifully written, with the inclusion of poems from mother and daughter, it tugged at my heart, made me laugh, infuriated me, and gave me deeper and richer understanding of what it's like to be in the world with a physical disability. I applaud these two strong women for their clarity, honesty and humor.

—Helene Simkin Jara, author of *Because I Had To* and the upcoming *True Doll Stories*

Tell Me the Number before Infinity *allowed me to walk into Becky and Dena's life, sit down at their kitchen table, and listen to their story firsthand. . . and what a story it is! This narrative is a gift for all allies of people with cerebral palsy. Teachers, parents, and counselors can use this book as a guide on the journey to make our spaces more welcoming, more supportive, more embracing of all of our "trailblazers."*

—Kathryn Harmon, Library Media Specialist

Quirky indeed! WILD indeed! Trailblazing disrupter Becky and her fiercely candid mama tell it like it really is. A heart-bopping, heart-stopping, thoughtful and poetic memoir. This family truly taught me what it meant to be an advocate for one's child. Undoubtedly my best math student ever, Becky arrived in my third-grade classroom and crashed into my heart forever. Her delight in each day was a lovely mix of a newborn's curiosity and the "knowing" of an old soul. Becky has achieved meaningful work for social justice, and the independence she always dreamed of. Becky and her mom have given us a compelling glimpse into their unconventional lives.

—Marcia Areias, Becky's third-grade teacher

Becky says that if she was born different than she was, she wouldn't think the way she does, and this is beautiful—important for everyone to think about. We experience the lives and feelings of these two wonderful women navigating all that happens together from birth through adulthood, from different viewpoints that are deeply intermingled. This is an important book. It carries strength, humor and pain, and it will make a profound difference in people's lives.

—Stan Rushworth, author of
Going to Water: The Journal of Beginning Rain

I feel as though I were invited into Becky's family. Dena shares such intimate feelings as she experiences the challenges of raising an independent-minded daughter with cerebral palsy. As a teacher, being a part of Becky's mathematical thinking is a rare treat. It's fun experiencing Becky analyze the world around her.

—Lynne Alper, mathematics educator

Tell Me the Number before Infinity

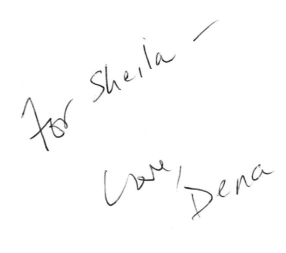

For Sheila —

Love, Dena

Other books by Dena Taylor

Red Flower: Rethinking Menstruation

Editor or co-editor of the following anthologies:

Disabled Mothers: Stories and Scholarship
by and about Mothers with Disabilities

Feminist Parenting: Struggles, Triumphs, & Comic Interludes

The Time of Our Lives: Women Write on Sex after 40

Sexual Harassment: Women Speak Out

Women of the 14th Moon: Writings on Menopause

Tell Me
the Number
before Infinity

The story of a girl with a quirky mind,
an eccentric family, and oh yes, a disability

by
Becky Taylor
and
Dena Taylor

MANY NAMES PRESS
CAPITOLA, CALIFORNIA

First Edition
ISBN 0-9773070-8-5 (ISBN-10)
ISBN 978-0-9773070-8-1 (ISBN-13)
(eBook ISBN 978-1-9444970-0-2 forthcoming)

Credits:
Cover photo: *Becky Taylor at 4* by Martin Taylor (Becky's grandfather)
Front Cover design by Janet Fine (with Becky's handwriting)
Back Cover photo by Julianna Hoffman
Sad Wait for Becky, photo by Leo Cohen
Anna's Play, by Anna (Taylor) Olausson
Math Winner, photo by Sam Vestal
Book design by Kate Hitt at Many Names Press

Many Names Press
P.O. Box 1038 Capitola, CA 95010 USA
Email: khitt@manynamespress.com

Library of Congress Cataloging-in-Publication Data

Names: Taylor, Becky, 1972- author. | Taylor, Dena, author.
Title: Tell me the number before infinity : the story of a girl with a quirky
    mind, an eccentric family, and oh yes, a disability / by Becky Taylor and
    Dena Taylor.
Description: First edition. | Capitola, California : Many Names Press, 2016.
Identifiers: LCCN 2016001109 (print) | LCCN 2016003357 (ebook) | ISBN
    9780977307081 (pbk. : alk. paper) | ISBN 0977307085 (pbk. : alk. paper) |
    ISBN 9781944497002 (e-book)
Subjects: LCSH: Taylor, Becky, 1972---Health. | Taylor, Dena. | Cerebral
    palsied--California--Biography. | Mother and child--California. | People
    with disabilities--Biography.
Classification: LCC RC388 .T39 2016 (print) | LCC RC388 (ebook) | DDC
    616.8/360092/2794--dc23
LC record available at http://lccn.loc.gov/2016001109

To Rodney

without whom this story wouldn't exist

And to Anna

for all the light she brings

Acknowledgments

We want to thank the No Name Writing Group of Santa Cruz, California, for its years of encouragement and critical feedback on our chapters. The members of that excellent collection of writers are Amber, Dee, Ellen, Ellie, Gail, Joan, Kim, Lillian, Susan, and Ziggy. We also very much appreciate Julianne Johnson for her important comments and Louise and Ralph Black for reading an early version of the book and telling us what they thought. Also many thanks to Julie Olsen Edwards, Stan Rushworth, Marcia Areias, and Lynne Alper for reading and giving valuable feedback. A thousand thank-yous to Kathryn Chetkovich for her editing expertise, to Kathie Hightower and Robin Atwood for all their help, and to Janet Fine for her artful eye. And a huge thank-you to Kate Hitt of Many Names Press for making this book a reality. And finally, we are grateful for all our friends and family for their love and support.

A slightly different version of "Riding Free" was previously published in *Woman of Power*, Issue 18, 1990. "Monsters" and "Pushing Me On" were previously published in *Phren-Z*; "Some People" and "Monsters" were previously published in *In Celebration of the Muse 15th Anniversary Anthology*.

Foreword

This is a memoir told from two perspectives. Our chapters are interwoven, and because they are chronological, there are more of the mother's, Dena's, at the beginning. Sometimes the same event is described by each of us from our separate points of view. Many of the pieces were written at the time they happened, as both of us are in the habit of writing things down. Some of Becky's pieces were originally done as school assignments. And some we wrote just to keep ourselves sane.

We have tried to be honest in our writing. Half of our family is here only in our telling, and in an excerpt from a play written by Becky's sister. They have their own stories.

We have put this book together so that parents, teachers, people with disabilities, and people who know people with disabilities can have a better understanding of the everyday life—the hard times and the humor—of a girl who is, indeed, a trailblazer.

—Becky Taylor and Dena Taylor

Table of Contents

Table of Contents, Continued

London, 1972
Dena

It is painful to think about Becky's birth, because it was then, most likely, that the damage occurred. The brain damage. I was living in London, working as a community organizer with a group of older women who had been "meths drinkers"—users of methylated spirits, a cheap and unhealthy form of alcohol—and an entire neighborhood that was being demolished to make room for public housing. I had moved to England in the late sixties after graduate school, and was now sharing a flat and my life with Rodney, an Englishman who was separated from his wife and two young children.

My parents were visiting from California, and they did not much care for my choice of a mate. We were all, however, excited about the pregnancy. When my water broke, at six-and-a-half months pregnant, Rodney had just moved out because of the terrible tension between the two of us. Was it our arguing that caused me to go into labor? Was it my parents' suitcases I'd been hauling around? Was it the sex we had just before Rodney left?

An ambulance delivered me to King's College Hospital, the biggest and best teaching hospital in London, where doctors gave me medications to stop the labor. My parents left that day to catch their plane back home. It was the end of their two-week visit. I was alone. "It does not look good," the doctors said. "This baby is too small to be born."

Many hours later, at 12:15am on August 4, this baby, who had been very active in the womb but was quiet now, entered the world, but did not start breathing. Maybe it was because of the drugs they administered; maybe it was because the cord was around her neck. The doctors let out audible groans, said it was a girl, and one of them whisked her to the other side of the room to try to resuscitate her. I learned later that he put a tube down her throat and blew his own breath into her for 25 minutes until she could breathe by herself. They took her to a neonatal unit and put me in a room with new moms who had just given birth to healthy babies. Hearing their conversations and seeing them nursing their newborns was excruciatingly painful.

I could not get any answers about my baby's condition or where she was, so I wandered the halls of that huge hospital looking for her, if indeed she was still alive. My first look at her was in the preemie ward, inside an incubator donated by Princess Margaret. Several tubes were attached to her body, and a huge needle went into her head. She was just skin and bones, too young for any muscle, two pounds ten ounces, but with a full head of dark hair and deep purple eyes. The nurses explained that the feeding tube was in her head because that was how they could reach the biggest vein. There was also a monitor under her that would set off an alarm if she stopped breathing, prompting a nurse to rush over and pull a string that jiggled her foot, reminding her to take a breath. It was a common thing, they said, for babies this premature to forget to breathe. I was not allowed to hold her. Her condition was critical, and they didn't know if she'd make it. I could, however, put my finger through a hole into the incubator. She grabbed it and stared at me and I talked to her.

One doctor told me a few hours later to get pregnant again right away, because my baby, if she lived, was probably going to be blind, deaf, and retarded. Shocked at everything he said, I could only glare at him.

Rodney returned a few days later. I spent most of my time at the hospital. The staff set up a bed for me so I could stay at night. All the mothers who had preemies pumped their breast milk which was then mixed together and fed to the babies. After a few days the nurses told me I'd better give the baby a name, because it looked like she was going to live, and they needed to know what to call her. We had thought to name her after Rodney's mother, Sarah, but that didn't seem to fit anymore. This baby needed a plucky name. Becky.

It was twelve days before I could hold her in my arms, and two months before I could take her home. Take her home I did, when she was four months old, all the way to California. When I got off the plane in San Francisco with a baby and my guitar, some people thought I was Joan Baez.

Two Babies
Dena

I watched Becky's development carefully the first months of her life. I knew early on that she wasn't blind or deaf, and she seemed very alert. She didn't sit up or crawl when she should have, but the doctors said because she was so premature, she would be slow at those things anyway. Rodney (who had followed me to California) and I played with her, talked to her, read to her, took her everywhere.

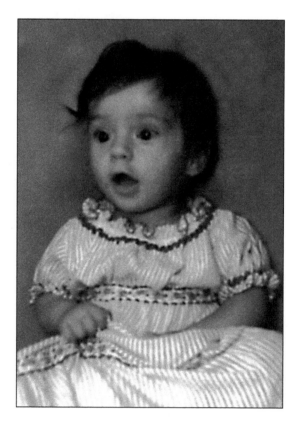

At fourteen months, a doctor told me she had cerebral palsy, and that there was no way of telling what her life would be like. He said CP is a disorder with a wide range of symptoms, from slight to severe. I was three months pregnant with Anna.

I made a promise to myself that I would be very careful during this pregnancy and not be as active as I was with Becky, in case that had anything to do with her being born prematurely. I breathed easier each new day after the six-and-a-half-month mark. Anna was born full-term on Easter Sunday. The hospital dressed her in a pink bunny suit which Rodney cut the ears off of as soon as we got home, saying it was a silly American custom.

We moved to Canada when Anna was six weeks old. Rodney's sister lived in Alberta, and had a friend who owned a cabin in a remote area in the foothills of the Rockies. In exchange for rent, we had to make sure water kept running into a trough for the cattle. There was a wood stove for heating the house. One autumn morning when I went upstairs to get the girls, their diapers were frozen to their bottoms. That's it, I said, we're going back to California.

I watched Anna's development as closely as I watched Becky's. As she grew, she soon surpassed what Becky could do physically. When Anna started walking, Becky, twenty months older, was still crawling. She could pull herself up to standing, but her balance was unsteady and her left hamstring muscle was tight. She could feed herself, but it was messy. She could talk, slowly, and she could definitely think, quickly.

The girls were very close and played together constantly. Rodney built them a treehouse not too far off the ground so Becky could climb into it too, and made a store out of a huge cardboard box with a little chair in it so that Becky could sit.

Becky seemed very matter-of-fact about what she couldn't do. I overheard this conversation once:

Becky: "Anna, let's play a game."

Anna: "No. I don't want to play a game. I want to play running."

Becky: "Okay, then I'll play a game while you play running."

Another time, when we were getting ready to go to my parents' house, Anna, age four, said, "I'll carry the book."

"I'll carry the bag," Becky said. Then, out loud but to herself, she said, "Well, that would mean someone would have to carry me *and* the bag. I'll have to wait until I can walk." As it happened, she took her first step by herself, without her walker, soon after this. Later she drew a picture titled, "A lady in a long dress walking out of a store carrying heavy bags."

I found things with the girls usually worked out best if I didn't interfere. One day while playing in the backyard, Anna asked Becky to go in the house and get the scissors. I heard this, and wasn't thrilled at the idea of Becky going down the stairs, unsteady, holding on to the banister, with the scissors, but didn't say anything. Becky then told Anna that she couldn't do it because "her Bubba didn't want her to go." Who was this Bubba, I wondered?

I also wondered how I was going to manage protecting Becky, letting her take care of herself, and getting her whatever help was available. All this and not slight Anna.

Starting School
Dena

As a friendly three-year-old, and the only one in her pre-school class who could speak, Becky was taken out of her school for handicapped children and placed into a Head Start program. It was 1975 and California had recently passed a law making public education available to all children regardless of handicap, and that meant government-funded schools had to integrate disabled children into their programs. They wanted Becky.

The teachers and aides, however, were a bit skeptical. This was new to them and they were not trained to work with children with disabilities. I met with them several times during Becky's first days to assure them she would not be a problem in the class. Rodney

Santa Cruz Head Start children involved in play activities.

told her as she left for school on the bus one day, "Don't take any shit from those teachers!" Thereafter Anna, age two, said to Becky every morning, "Don't take any shit to those teachers!" Head Start was, all in all, a good experience for Becky. She was cheerful when she left in the morning, and cheerful still when the bus brought her home.

Kindergarten, the following year, did not start well. The school officials told us Becky could attend only one hour a day because they insisted she needed a full-time aide, and the school could only afford an aide for one hour. Becky wanted to go full time. We saw no reason why she shouldn't, and it was the law. We protested to the district officials to no avail. Becky was interviewed on a San Francisco TV station and our local paper wrote up the story, with the headline "Sad Wait for Becky." We taped the article to our refrigerator and Anna, then three, would point to it and say "sadwaitforBecky, sadwaitforBecky."

Still, the school wouldn't change its decision, so the county paid for Becky to go to a school of our choice. We chose Montessori. She had been there for a year and a half when Rodney and I decided to teach both girls at home for a while. It seemed a good idea at the time. We thought we could give them a broader education: math, English, cooking, plants and animals of the beach, French, art and music, and of course, field trips. Rodney, well qualified for this (he'd been a teacher, a translator, a writer, guitarist, and cook), provided most of the instruction while I plugged away at my home business. I was "The Village Typist," busy editing and typing papers and dissertations for college students.

After a while, working at home and teaching two kids at home, when home was a two-room apartment, didn't seem like such a good idea. We moved to another school district by the time Becky was ready for second grade. She entered the public school with no problems; she seemed well-adjusted, making some friends during that year.

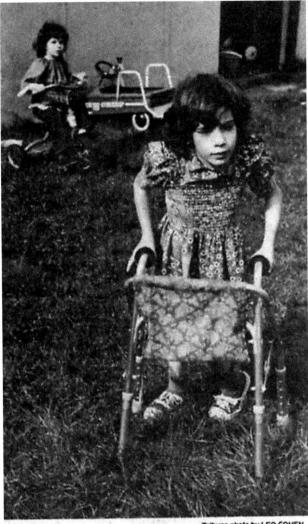

Tribune photo by LEO COHEN

5-YEAR-OLD BECKY STRULO-TAYLOR
She would love to attend school full time

Tell Me the Number before Infinity
Dena

We first became aware of Becky's mathematical ability when she was four years old. Rodney and I were going to make our own candles for our Hanukkah menorah and were talking about how many we would need—one the first night, two the second, and so on for eight nights, plus a shamus candle every night for lighting the others. Becky looked up at us and said, "You need 44 altogether." We looked at her, looked at each other, knelt down close and asked her how she knew that.

"One night when I was lying in bed I figured out how to do that sort of problem," she told us. We recognized it as a sum-of-a-series problem, not the usual fodder for a four-year-old's mind. "It's calculus," my brother John said when I told him. From that day on, Becky astounded us all by figuring out complicated mathematical functions in her head. She could multiply two three-digit numbers faster than my father could get the answer on his calculator.

Not long after this—Becky was still four—she and Rodney were having one of their playful discussions about numbers. Becky had a comeback to all of the questions he put to her. Finally he asked, "Okay, Smartypants, here's one for you: Is infinity an odd or an even number?" She thought about this for a bit, smiled, then said to her dad, "Tell me the number before infinity."

I remember a time when she was in first grade, and Rodney asked her, "What is 346 times 12?"

"I'd have to figure it out... It's 4,152."

"How did you do that?"

"I took half of 346 which is 173, and added it on. That makes 519, right? Then I double it and that makes times 3, right? Then I multiply that times 2 and then I multiply that times 2."

"Look at what they give her in school," Rodney said to me, and handed me a sheet with 3+2, 6+1, 5+2.

At six, Becky told Rodney and me, "I know what my dreams will be." She told Rodney she was going to have a dream about a picture that was made of tiny dots of every color, and the next morning she said she did dream it. She said that in between her dreams there are little pictures about the end of the next dream.

She told me one day while she was undressing for a bath, "My mind knows everything. It even knows the plan for the last day of the world."

"Really? What *is* the plan?"

"I haven't asked my mind yet," she said. "I have to do it at a different time."

From about age seven, Becky always balanced my checkbook. She was great to shop with because she could figure out the best buys in an instant, and she was quite useful in a restaurant when it was time to divide the bill or figure out the tip. In school, she was always put into the highest math class, and every year she won first, second or third place for her grade in the county math contest. Since she had difficulty writing, the test officials provided her with a "writer" who put Becky's answers on the test. She never used the scratch paper that was provided; she did it all in her head.

Independence
Dena

At four-and-a-half years old, Becky was ready for a walker. She could now stand up and go places on her own. The whole family had been eagerly awaiting this. My grandmother Eda, an expert seamstress, made her a green-and-purple bag similar to the one she had on her own walker so that Becky could carry things, such as toys and, later, school supplies.

Our first outing was to Dossett Brothers, the little grocery store on the corner. We got out of the car, I handed Becky her walker, and she went in by herself for the very first time. I followed her through the door, watchful, proud, and close to tears. Before this day she had always been in her stroller. Her face beamed with excitement and confidence. In the store she could go wherever *she* wanted. She headed straight for the refrigerator bins, at her chest level, and looked down at all the food. With a huge grin, she picked out some cheese, butter, and salami and placed them in our shopping cart. I, too, could hardly contain my joy as we slowly walked up and down the aisles picking out things to buy.

As we were standing at the checkout counter, a woman turned to stare at Becky and said, loudly, "Eeeew, is he going to have to walk like that all his life?" I glared at her, wanting to scream at her, wanting, really, to grab and shake her, but also wanting to say something to make Becky feel okay. As calmly as I could, but loudly, I said, "SHE just got her walker and this is her FIRST TIME OUT WITH IT."

Not long after that, Becky was invited to her first non-family birthday party. It was for Lindsey, a friend from school. I took Becky to the party and stayed by her the whole time, even though Lindsey's mother said it was fine if I left. Becky's walker was still new to her, and I was worried about how she'd do in a crowd of kids. Thinking about it later, I felt very foolish and told myself I really must try and not be so over-protective.

Her second party soon followed, this time for Twila, another school friend. Becky talked to her on the phone about it, then I spoke to Twila's mother, who said she was taking the children to see *Pinocchio,* and afterwards to a park for a picnic. Becky was very excited. Rodney and I, however, wondered about several things: Should we go with her? How would she get from her seat in the movie to the car? And Becky had never been to a movie theater before; would the noises startle her, as loud noises sometimes did?

We asked Becky what she would like to do and how much she wanted our help. "I want to walk with my walker and do it all myself," she told us. We only needed to take her to the movie and pick her up afterwards at the park. Remembering the Lindsey party, I thought we should do what she wanted. Thankfully, we did. She could not stop smiling as we drove home from the park.

The Kind of Person She Is
Dena

Rodney and I are snuggling in bed, talking. He's telling me about a music tape he's going to make at the radio station that afternoon, and how he'd like to take Anna with him. Not Becky and Anna, just Anna. Becky wouldn't be able to follow him around as Anna can. Anna is three, Becky is five.

And then it hits me, surges up from deep inside. A wrenching, terrible feeling, and I start to cry. This of course interrupts our mood. I blurt out, "I feel so bad that Becky isn't a normal kid!"

Rodney's reaction, which angers but doesn't surprise me, is to laugh derisively. "I guess you were a normal kid," he says, "to feel that way. I wasn't." He means he grew up in England, Jewish, during the war.

"It's not the same, and you know it." I tell him about what happened the day before. Walking a few yards behind him when he was pushing Becky in the stroller, I overheard some boys talking about her.

"Did you see that girl? She was blind," said one of the boys.

"I didn't know she was blind, but I knew she was fucked up."

In my mind, I shouted after them: She's *not blind! And…she's…not…fucked up.*

Rodney says, "Why didn't you talk to them? I would have."

"What would you have said?"

"I would have called them over and told them that she wasn't blind and she wasn't fucked up, and I would have told them a little bit about her."

"What would you have said about her?" I wanted to hear it myself.

"I would have told them how she was born prematurely, how she only had a one-in-three chance of living, how it could've happened to them or their sisters or brothers, and also could happen to their own children. I'd have said her muscles don't do what she wants them to, how she's taught herself to walk, and that it's probably as hard for her to walk on the playground as it is for them on top of a 20-foot wall. I'd have told them that she laughs and jokes just like they do. And then I'd have asked them if they'd like to come over and have tea and meet her and see for themselves what kind of a person she is."

So when Becky started school, this is the sort of thing we said to her classmates every year until she told us she could do it herself.

Monsters

Dena

"There are monsters biting at my brain," Becky told us. She was five, maybe six. "They won't go away."

"At night? In your dreams?" I asked.

"No. In the day."

" *When* in the day?"

"Just sometimes in the day."

"What do they look like?"

"They have teeth all over."

"Can you tell them to go away?" I asked her. "I mean, look right at them and yell at them to get out of there?"

"I tried that. I even put up signs in my brain saying GO AWAY! FUCK OFF! CLOSED DOWN FOREVER! But it didn't do any good."

We were sitting at the kitchen table. Rodney and I looked at each other and burst out laughing. What a kid. Where did she get the idea to do that?

"Well, that certainly was a good try," I told her. I wondered if there was any connection between "biting her brain" and the fact that she is "brain damaged."

"Can you draw us a picture of one of the monsters?" Rodney asked her. We got her a pencil and paper and she drew a shape with teeth all over it. She said the monsters were white.

"I have an idea," Rodney said. "Let's make some cookies that look like your monsters. Then, every time they come into your head, you can take a cookie and eat it. Shall we do that?"

Becky considered this plan, and said yes. So Rodney made some cookie dough and cut out monster shapes using Becky's drawing. Then he put cornflakes all over them for the teeth, and put them in the oven to bake. When the monster cookies were cool, we put them in a big glass jar on a low shelf so Becky could reach them.

A few days later, she took a cookie and ate it. The monsters never came back. We finally threw the moldy cookies out.

Figuring It Out
Dena

When Becky was young, Rodney and I sought out as many adults with cerebral palsy as we could. We wanted to find out from them what their parents or care-givers did that they wished they had not done, or what they wished had happened that didn't. We also wanted to see how these adults felt about various types of physical therapy and surgeries they'd had.

With one exception, every adult we talked to hated physical therapy. They felt there was way too much emphasis on it, that it took up great amounts of time and was not very beneficial. It was the same with surgeries: they were done for the parents' benefit, so that the parents could feel they were doing something, or so their kid would look a little more "normal." The lone believer was a man who had had years of physical therapy and extensive surgery on his legs. He felt it had been worthwhile, even though he missed two years of school and was still in pain.

With other parents, we started a group for those of us who had kids with disabilities so we could talk about our concerns and help each other. Most of these parents we met when Becky was attending the Duncan Holbert School for Handicapped Children when she was three. Rodney and I also wrote to organizations in other countries to see what they did for children with cerebral palsy. We received a letter from a rehabilitation treatment center in Moscow (translated by a teacher of Russian at our local community college) saying they rarely did surgery on mild to moderate cases of CP, and only in 20% of severe cases.

We had seriously considered surgery on Becky's left leg to loosen the hamstring muscle. When she was six, we went to a series of appointments with doctors to determine whether she should have the surgery at that point. If so, she would not be starting school the next month.

"Well, Becky," said the doctor, "will you be going to school in the fall?" How could he ask such a ridiculous question, knowing it depended on the surgery decision? Becky looked right at him. "Probably and probably not," she told him. Later, when Rodney and I jokingly repeated this conversation to Moshe Feldenkrais, the founder of the Feldenkrais Method of bodywork, he looked at us, made a gesture to include all his students standing nearby, and said, "She's smarter than everyone else in this room."

We decided to schedule the operation even though, after much research, we still wondered if it was the right thing to do. It seemed as if it might help Becky to walk more easily, but we'd heard of hamstring surgeries where the leg then bent backwards and was left considerably weaker. So when the doctor casually told us during one of the pre-operative appointments that Becky would have casts on both legs, we balked. "Well," he said, "we might as well do them both, since she'll be under anesthesia." That's when we decided to reconsider the whole thing, and eventually chose not to have the surgery at all.

I still don't know if that was the right decision.

Small Talk
Becky

My mommy and daddy just spent a long time discussing with the doctors a possible surgery to loosen my extra-tight left-leg muscles. I am six years old. One of the doctors turns to me and asks, "So Becky, are you going to go to school in the fall?"

All eyes turn to me.

"Probably," I say, thinking of the struggle to get me into the right school.

It was my choice to go to a public school instead of one for kids with disabilities, but the public school didn't want me to go all day. A TV crew had recently interviewed my parents about this disagreement. The night the interview aired, my family (and some friends) went to another friend's house to watch it. I was shown walking around with my walker while my parents were interviewed.

Then, suddenly, I look at the doctor, and think, if I have the surgery, I'll be in the hospital come fall. "And probably not," I tell him.

As it turned out, at the next appointment we discovered that the surgeons were planning on operating on both my legs, not just one, and my parents said no.

So I went to school after all.

Weight Lifting
Dena

I started having little pains in my side and back as Becky got bigger, and found myself feeling worried about getting older and not being able to carry her much longer. Then I met Mary. She had a daughter named Lisa who went to Becky's pre-school, and Lisa, like Becky, had cerebral palsy.

It was "graduation day" for the kids. There was a potluck picnic for the children and parents in a park. Becky was using her walker, and she and I ambled at our snail's pace across the park while most of the other kids ran on ahead. Mary and Lisa passed us, Mary holding Lisa's hand and urging her to hurry. Finally, impatient, she lifted Lisa up and carried her. Looking over her shoulder at me, she called out, "Well, there's one thing about having a kid with CP, it sure has made my back strong!" I looked at Mary, smaller than I am, and I looked at Lisa, bigger than Becky. Months passed before I realized that those words had changed my attitude.

I started paying more attention to the ways I was lifting and carrying Becky, and it got easier and easier. My pains went away. By the time Becky was six years old, I was lifting and carrying her with no problem, and I felt strong. I thought of it as a kind of weightlifting.

Rice for Dinner
Becky

One evening, when I was four years old and taking a bath, my dad burst in and asked me, "What's one-and-a-half times one-and-a-half?" "Two-and-a-quarter," I answered behind him as he left (satisfied) for the kitchen. This question must have been a regular occurrence because I knew right away that he was measuring out the water for white rice and so we were going to be having rice for dinner.

My Dad and I had regular discussions throughout my early childhood about math and ideas. He read Edwin Abbott's 1884 book, *Flatland* (about encountering a different dimension), to me, and we did some of the exercises together. We also read other books about math and logic. And we made Mobius strips by taking a long rectangular piece of paper and putting a twist in it before connecting the ends. (When you draw a line through the middle of it, before you get back to your starting point, you'll have marked both sides of the paper.) One time, he told me abruptly that, "The reason I spent so much time teaching you math is because I thought you were going to be in a wheelchair." This surprised me in a not-very-nice way.

I was balancing the family checkbook by the time I was eight years old. At the grocery store, I was often asked, "What's a better deal?"

I would race my grandfather in multiplication problems as a kid. Me in my head and him on the calculator. I'd multiply numbers together by first factoring them and then multiplying the factors together in descending order. For example if asked, "What's 441 times 732?" I would first find all of the prime factors for both of them, 441=7 x 7 x 3 x 3 and 732=61 x 3 x 2 x 2. Then 61 x 7 x 7 x 3 x 3 x 3 x 2 x 2 = 322,812. The hardest and most frustrating part for me came next: saying it out loud. I have a stutter that often prevents me from saying clearly what I'm thinking. When I'm saying words, I can sometimes trick my stutter by saying it in another way, but I can't do this with numbers.

My fourth-grade teacher gave students who learned their times tables the option of a ride in his airplane. His definition of learning was that you should get the answers down on paper fast. It has always been hard for me to write fast and legibly. So, one day, he gave me two three-digit numbers and asked me to multiply them in my head. When I told him the correct product, he took my whole family up to see our house from the air.

Every Crumb of Every Minute of Every Day
Becky

I have fond memories of living in those colorful houses on Capitola beach. I was seven and Anna was six when we first moved there. It was a great place to be a kid. We lived there in the off-season for a few years, moving out in the summer when the rents went up. We always found a good place to stay. Besides the beach, we could play in the neighborhood with other kids. There was a large protected area between the houses, away from cars. Anna got a pair of roller skates. (I had to try out those skates one day!) I had a big tricycle, and we would load the basket with groceries and other things from the car, and I would take them to our door. This made me feel useful.

At Montessori school, the kindergarten class was in a room all to itself, but first through third graders were all together. Anna tried their preschool and quit. Because I got personal attention, I thrived in kindergarten, but first grade was different. I felt lost in such a big class.

One day, the first graders had a party to show our parents what we had learned in swim class. My mother was there on the sidelines. All the kids were in the water when the teacher told me to hold on to the side of the pool. There wasn't enough there for me to hold on to. So, my whole body slipped under the water. My mother was the one who jumped in and saved me from drowning. Our whole family was disappointed with Montessori school, and I didn't want to go back.

At this time, our parents decided they could give us a better education than we were getting at school. So, they homeschooled us for about a year. I liked being homeschooled. This was a time when my mother was the wage earner for the family. With our dad, we would do various school-like activities, such as coloring pictures of the layers in the earth according to how hot they are. We kept a binder with our work. I had a math tutor from the local community college. A neighbor from that time recently told me that she remembers the tutor talking about some math concept and saying, "I never really understood that, but now I do."

Even before we moved to the beach, my mother started teaching Anna and me how to touch-type and where the keys were. Anna would go around the house saying "A-S-D-F-J-K-L-semicolon-X-Y-Z" as if that were the alphabet. When she tried to add A-B-C, it didn't work so well. With me, I learned where the keys were, but I have to look down to see where my hands are. Keyboarding, for me, is easier and faster and more legible than handwriting, but I'm not as fast as other people.

Here are some examples of my typing when I was five and six. (Eda was my great-grandmother.)

```
                                  July 4, 1988


Dear Eda,

    I hope it's nice in the hospital and if not

I hope you get out of it soon.It!s very exciting

this summer especially for me because we're going

up to aan Francisco for exercises and because

I'm learning to type & this is my third letter

X I typed.

                        Love

                        Becky
```

```
Mommy making  breakfast and just about ready to   put
eggs in the bowl with her hands and face red from an
argument wearing her stripedd housedress and her hair
thing withx them stdixxxxxxxxxxx stick  vis ible
before she gg gotxx her red Birkenstocks...

                              10/24/78
```

In the middle of the next school year, Anna and I entered the
local elementary school. She was in first grade and I was in second.
Sometimes Anna and my dad would walk to school together along
the railroad tracks. I knew that it would have been impossible for
me to do this walk, so I was happy that my mother drove me.

I remember coming home on some winter days and seeing
storm barriers of wood nailed to the bottom of the doorway with
sandbags in front of them. That was how close we were to the
ocean. On especially stormy nights, Anna and I were taken up to
our grandparents' house in the hills.

Every spring, Capitola had a kite festival. I don't think we
entered any kites, but I was good at, and enjoyed, untangling
string. It was something that my unpredictable body could easily
do because it didn't take much movement and even if my arms
jerked around, my hands were still stuck in the string.

When we moved to the first of the three places we lived in near
the beach, we were trying to go to Israel so I could have regular
sessions with Moshe Feldenkrais. We didn't go, but if we had, none
of us knew when we would actually leave. One day my parents
seemed especially worried about our potential trip, so I, thinking

about the beauty of our surroundings, told them, "Enjoy every crumb of every minute of every day!"

My mother seemed to take this advice to heart, because one morning not long after that, she called to Anna and me to "hurry up and see the sunrise." I can't move fast, particularly in the mornings, and I fell and bruised my bottom on the bedpost. I couldn't see much of anything through my tears that morning and had to sit on cushions and soft surfaces until my tailbone healed. I wondered about kids who are spanked repeatedly. Our parents never spanked Anna or me.

The lesson I carried forward from that day is that it's not worth hurrying. My mental shorthand still is: A sunrise isn't worth a fall.

Let Me Tell You about the Mother

Dena

Sometimes I get so frustrated
Everything I do with her
takes forever
But what is time
and why does it matter
The people we meet say
What a lovely girl
but they look at us pityingly
when we walk
down the street
Why don't people talk
regular
Don't have to shout
Don't have to direct questions
to me, the mother
I'm fed up with *how old is she*
ASK HER FOR CHRISSAKE

Yesterday she fell on my guitar
and broke it
I was pissed off
Told her so
Then felt guilty
Then thought: what the hell
I'd feel bad whoever did it
We talked about it
She knew what I meant
She always knows

Let me tell you about the mother
I hurt every time she falls
and she falls a lot
I hurt every time people look at her
with that funny look
And I say fuck them
And I gather her in my arms
kiss her and say
I love you Becky
and she says I love you Mom
I want to take her away
But where?
This is where we live
This is where we do
our daily stuff
Often we cry
and often we laugh
This is our life

A Funny Encounter
Becky

A while ago, I was taking a walk in the tourist town where I live. I noticed a boy walking with the same kind of crutches that I have. These are a new type of lightweight crutches. I said "hi" and so did he. Then he noticed the crutches and said to his mother, "Mine are pink and hers are blue." Then we moved on, each going our separate ways.

Odd Ones Out

Dena

Eleven-year-old Becky sits at the kitchen table reading an article about herself in our local newspaper. The headline is *Math Winner: Doing It the Hard Way.*

"I wonder why they say that?" Becky muses.

"Probably because the writer believes that most people think doing complicated math problems in your head is harder than using a paper and pencil to get the answer," I tell her.

"Well, I think it's easier," she says.

The article tells how Becky placed first in her grade in our county's annual math contest. There is a picture of her smiling widely (which her orthodontist put on his wall because he was so pleased she was wearing her retainer). One of the questions on the test was "Add the following and give your answer in lowest terms: four and two-thirds, seven and five-twelfths, one and seventeen-eighteenths." The writer wonders if Becky is a mathematical genius or whether she has trained her mind to do things her fingers cannot. One thing I know is that when Becky was a baby in her crib, before she knew what her fingers could or could not do, I heard her saying to herself, "odd…even…odd…even…"

We didn't have a television in those days. What we had were books and elaborate family dinners prepared by Rodney. Once, at Parents' Night for Anna's class, the teacher motioned us over to Anna's desk and said, "Look at this." She had asked the children to write down their favorite meal, and while most kids wrote hamburgers or mac & cheese, Anna wrote, "A seven-course French dinner."

Math winner: doing it the hard way

Photo by Sam Vestal

House Aspirin
Becky

In the door frame of our back door, there are the marks of two teeth. These teeth belong to me. One evening, I tripped on the leg of a chair. I didn't hurt myself in this fall, but it left a permanent mark in our wall. My mother asked me, "Did you hurt yourself? Would you like an aspirin?" After I told her I was unhurt, we joked that the house must need a pain reliever.

The next day, I was showing off to my good friend. We were on our way outside when I stopped her. "Would you like to see something?" I asked, and showed her the marks. She was amazed. I have made dents in the furniture as well.

Patience
Dena

I am more patient now, entering middle age, than I ever was. I have learned to wait. In fact, I don't wait any more. I think of that waiting time as an extra bonus, and fill it with something that I like to do, often just stopping to close my eyes and breathe deeply. Then, when Becky's ready, we do whatever it is we had planned to do together.

It was not always this way. When Becky was young, I would get frustrated at how long everything took. I knew of course that she had to learn how to do things, no matter how long it took, and no matter if they could be done by someone else in a fraction of the time. When she first started doing the dishes it took her two hours, and vacuuming or changing her sheets took forever.

Speaking was also slow and difficult for Becky, but I made a point of never letting a thing she said to me go unacknowledged. If I didn't understand her words I'd ask her to use different ones until I could make out what she was saying. Years later, a speech therapist told me I shouldn't have done that because she needed to practice the sounds that were hard for her. Maybe he was right. She did develop a large vocabulary, however.

One day she said something that startled me. "I like to do things as slowly as possible," she told me. I had never before considered that someone would enjoy doing things slowly. It made me think hard about the way most of us rush through everything, from dressing to doing the dishes to driving to the store. Particularly driving. Even when I wasn't late or in a hurry, I'd drive as fast as I could get away with. Not anymore. Now when I'm stopped at a traffic light, I take time to look around, breathe, and if there's someone else in the car with me, give them my full attention.

Once a week the girls and I would have a one-hour cleaning

session. We'd put on some lively music and do as much as we could in our allotted time. Anna and I would rush around like a couple of wild women and Becky would calmly plug away at one or two things. At the end of the hour, we had all done our best, and the house was clean.

Halley's Comet came around when Becky was 13 and Anna's twelfth birthday was approaching. I woke the girls up three nights in a row in the middle of the night and we walked at Becky's slow pace out to the end of the wharf near our house, patiently waiting for a look at this phenomenon that I wanted them to see; they might not ever have a chance again. We never saw it there, but a day or two later, on Anna's birthday, when she had some friends over to spend the night, I piled them all into the car when it was very late and we went to another spot. And there, indeed, we saw the comet.

I Chose Taylor because
It Was a Common Name
Becky

When I entered junior high, my parents asked my sister and me what last names we wanted on our school records. Before this point, it had always been Strulo-Taylor. I was getting tired of having a name that people hadn't heard of. Most people would ask me to repeat it. Then they would ask me to spell it. For someone who talked with a stutter, this was often hard to do. On the school worksheets I remember there were 10 boxes in which to put your last name. I don't remember what I did with my 13 characters.

With all this to consider, I chose Taylor to be on my forms. Anna said that she wanted Strulo as her school name. I think she had many reasons to be a Strulo. One of them was that she wanted a name that was unusual. She also felt that she needed her own identity apart from me. Anna was known as my sister. She wasn't appreciated for who she was. A common thing about being a younger sibling is that teachers judge you by the older family members.

The big irony of this whole name thing is that by taking my mother's name, I'm the one who did the unusual thing. I have talked to Anna about this. Neither one of us thought about whose feelings we might be hurting. We were eleven and twelve at the time.

Around the same time, my father was talking about making up a last name. All of us would share that name. I wasn't particularly fond of having a made-up name. I don't know what the other family members thought, but I was already feeling too different to have a made-up last name. The only name that I can remember him suggesting is Bard. Bard was a possibility because it contained the first initials of all of our first names.

Strulo was already a made-up name. My grandfather had shortened it from Strulovichi. The new version didn't have any roots or family attached to it.

What's In a Name?
Dena

Soon after Rodney and I split up, when the girls were in 6th and 7th grade, Anna told me she was changing her name from Strulo-Taylor to Strulo. (I had long since reverted to just using Taylor, not liking the complexity of a hyphenated name, thus beginning the erosion of our combined-name idea.) I imagined that part of this was Anna's way of getting back at me for the break-up, but also sensed that it was a way for her to separate herself from Becky.

Becky's reaction was, "Well, if you're going to be Strulo, I'm going to be Taylor." The two of them had always been close, perhaps too close, and I thought some space might be a good thing. I told them to think about whether they'd like to go to different schools now, and if so, I would be happy to drive them. They quickly said no, that wasn't what they wanted. Anna said that she just wanted a different name. So Becky and I were Taylors and Anna was Strulo until she entered college, when she again added Taylor to her name.

Junior High Days
Becky

I have a memory of my friend and me, just the two of us, sitting on my bed discussing the classes and teachers. Kimi was a year older than I was, so she was able to tell me what to expect and who to avoid. We had known each other since I was in second grade. We kept in touch and went to each other's birthday parties. At one point Kimi's brother delivered our newspaper. She was my first long-time friend.

Seventh grade started out to be one of my best school years! It seemed my mother had been correct in her prediction: "Things will get better as you get older." For the first time, I had a choice in my classes. My teachers were, for the most part, understanding and even interested in different ways of problem-solving.

My math teacher was going to try to get me in the highest class at the school. There would be only one other seventh-grader in this honors class. My electives were art and computer programming. I appreciated the way that the computer teacher was open to my suggestions. Sometimes while he was lecturing, I would be programming in my head and talk to him about it after class. I was also enjoying my other classes.

Another plus was that I was re-connecting with friends from previous schools. At the beginning of the year, I had a choice of eating and associating with two groups of friends. I chose the one with Kimi.

After a month, some of the joy began to wear off. My physical education teacher was afraid I would hurt myself or wouldn't be able to participate in an activity. So, without checking with me, she decided that my physical activity for the rest of the year would consist of walking around the track with another student from the class. I don't know how she came up with the list of who accompanied me on which days. This teacher was the same one who, when I first came, told the whole class, "We need to accept everyone, because we are all different." I was also having trouble getting across the school from my art class to my algebra class in the time allowed. And my group of friends broke up.

On one particular day, a group of other students, including a boy from my previous school, started following me around and teasing me. They all shouted "Hey Becky, Hey Becky!" over and over across the schoolyard without giving me a chance to respond. This teasing hit me particularly hard, because I didn't know what it meant for my future. I had been under the impression that once people knew me, as did this boy who was at the front of the shouters, they wouldn't tease me. I now had to revise this belief.

Later that year, as this teasing continued, I went to my English teacher and asked her if she would mediate between me and the boys. She agreed and all of us talked. I thought it was resolved, but then they started again. When my English teacher saw us on her steps, the boys would deny it or say that they thought I had trouble hearing. This would make me very angry. And the next day or month it would happen again. I was the scapegoat for their anger at the school, their classes, or a number of other things.

On the day that the shouting started, my mother picked me up after school. I was so upset about what the boys did that we decided to get an ice cream before going home. We parked in a disabled parking place and I put up the temporary disabled-parking placard sent to us after my other one had been stolen out of our car.

When we got back to the car, there was a ticket on the window.

The Ticket
Dena

I picked up Becky after school, and she looked to be on the verge of tears. It could have been a problem with other kids, or her teachers, or perhaps she had fallen. She was obviously feeling very low, and this depressed me as well. I thought she could do with some cheering up, so we stopped to have an ice cream sundae and talk about what had happened.

When we got back to the car, I had a $50 ticket for having an expired disabled-parking placard. I flipped out. All the frustrations of the day, previous days, in fact *years* of frustrations, welled up and boiled over.

I drove straight to the police station and demanded to talk to someone about the ticket. Never mind that the placard actually *had* expired. That wasn't the point. Somewhat hysterical, I spewed forth a stream of words informing the startled officer of all the things that had happened to Becky that day at school, several things that had happened to her in the past years at school, that I had stopped to buy her an ice cream to try and make her feel better after this horrible day, and that in fact I had long since mailed in the paperwork for the new placard, it just hadn't arrived yet. I stopped only when he held the ticket in front of my eyes and said, "Look, lady, look, LOOK," and tore it in two.

The Only Operation
Dena

Once when Becky was ten I watched her try to open a door without even looking at the doorknob. I asked her why she felt around for the knob with her hand instead of using her eyes. She considered this and told me, "My body acts as if my mind thinks I'm blind."

Becky had strabismus, or crossed eyes, since birth. Rodney and I talked to several ophthalmologists when she was young about the possibilities for correcting this. We were told over and over that an operation could be performed for cosmetic reasons only, that she would never be able to see out of both eyes simultaneously – meaning she'd never have binocular vision or depth perception – and that the surgery might have to be redone two or three times because her eyes could revert to their crossed state.

We decided against this surgery, or surgeries, and thought we would let Becky herself decide later if she wanted to have it done for cosmetic reasons.

In the meantime, I sent away for various eye exercise programs, and Becky and I did these over the years. Nothing worked to straighten her eyes.

When she was fourteen, I was helping her with metaphors and similes for her English class. She was supposed to write "My eyes are..."

"Windows," she said, "because you can see out of them."

"And also you can see into them," I said. "You can tell a lot about a person by looking into their eyes."

"You can?" she asked.

Wow, I thought. Becky is so accustomed to people not looking her in the eye when they talk to her, because her eyes are crossed (I've watched it happen; they look away), that she does not look people in the eye herself. She doesn't realize that's what people do in this society. So I explained to her how important it is, and told her over and over, "Look me in the eye!" whenever she talked to me.

Shortly after this, Becky decided she wanted her eyes to be straight. She and I went to many eye doctors, seeking the latest information. We were given the same answers we had encountered years earlier, but this time the doctors really angered me because they talked only to me, not to Becky. She'd get up in the examination chair and say, "I have strabismus and I want to talk about having it corrected," and the doctor would turn away from her and talk to me.

A friend gave us the name of an optician who supposedly was the best in the area. She examined Becky's eyes, said no amount of exercise would straighten them, and told us about an eye surgeon in San Francisco whose specialty was correcting strabismus.

I sat with Becky in Dr. Jampolsky's waiting room and looked around at the many mothers and children. It looked like a collection of United Nations families. The woman next to me said she lived in southern California, and had taken her son back to her native England to have his eyes operated on for free under the national health program, only to be told that the best surgeon in the world for this operation was in San Francisco.

Dr. Jampolsky examined Becky's eyes for a long time, spoke directly to her, and answered our questions. He said he was amazed that her vision was good in both eyes, that usually with this condition a child will stop using one eye and the vision in that eye will deteriorate and eventually be gone. Maybe all my years of covering Becky's eyes one at a time and having her tell me what she could see had something to do with it, or perhaps it was Becky's habit of using one eye, then the other, when she was looking at something (causing her head to move around a lot).

A date was set for the surgery. On the way home we went over everything the doctor had said. I told Becky I didn't understand why she wouldn't have binocular vision after the surgery. Dr. Jampolsky had developed a method of lining the eyes up perfectly, and her vision was good in both eyes, so why not? She didn't understand either, but every other doctor had told us this was impossible. In any case, Becky wanted to have the surgery done so her eyes would be straight.

We made plans to be in San Francisco for two days, since the doctor needed to examine Becky the day after the surgery. Anna and my mother wanted to come with us. Anna, twelve then, was taking a very long time packing.

"What's happening?" I asked. "You don't need much for a two-day trip."

"I'm trying to find shirts with no writing on them," she explained, rummaging through all their t-shirts, "because Becky's not supposed to do any reading for a week."

We picked up my mother, drove to the city, got settled in our motel, and went to Becky's pre-surgery appointment. I told Dr. J. I didn't understand why Becky wouldn't have binocular vision after the operation. He answered simply, "She will."

In high spirits, we went out for dinner at a Chinese restaurant, with Becky joking about flames coming from the kitchen. We tried to get a good night's sleep with Anna and my mom in one bed, Becky and me in the other, and left early in the morning for the hospital.

Seeing your child wheeled into the operating room is terrible, the waiting endless. Finally, when it was over, a nurse asked if I could come to the recovery room. They were having trouble keeping Becky calm. She had torn her bandages off and was thrashing around. I went to her, told her where she was and that the operation was over, told her I would stay with her, and explained about the bandages. She relaxed and said she was sorry she had torn at the bandages. "Am I acting strange?" she asked, unable to see. "Not at all," I said.

I then found out that the anesthetic Becky had been given was not sodium pentothal, which a nurse had said would be used, and which I had had for a hernia operation when *I* was fourteen (and in fact told Becky that I rather liked). Instead they had used ether, which necessitated a mask over her mouth and nose. They told me later that the doctor insisted they use ether because it doesn't affect the eye muscles. But Becky had a hard time with the mask, particularly the feeling of not getting enough air. Maybe this had something to do with her breathing problems at birth. I told Becky I was really sorry that we had been given the wrong information about the type of anesthetic to be used. She had obviously been through a horrible ordeal going into and coming out of the surgery. The nurses told me she wouldn't remember any of this, and it seems they were right.

She was moved to another room, and Anna, my mother, and I sat with her as she gradually woke up. We were told that patients often feel nauseated after eye surgery, as it upsets their equilibrium, so we should watch to see that she didn't vomit (she did) and then choke. This was outpatient surgery, and nurses were scarce. We were sent home in the evening, one groggy patient and three exhausted attendants.

I carried Becky upstairs to our room in the motel (the elevator wasn't working!) and laid her carefully on her side in the bed she and I were sharing. Although both eyes had been operated on, only one was now bandaged, so she was able to see the balloons that Anna had bought for her. She soon went to sleep again. The rest of us were wrecks. We sat on the other bed and ate the sandwiches the nurses had given us and opened the bottle of Irish whiskey I had bought while Becky was in surgery. Later, I climbed in next to Becky and held her. I listened to her breathing all night long.

It wasn't until after the surgery that Becky told me of her dreams before the operation. "They were upsetting," she said.

"They were showing my nervousness. During the conscious day I wasn't aware of being afraid, but I kind of knew that it was there somewhere. Like dreaming about going to school blind."

In the morning when she started to wake up I asked how she was feeling. "All right," she said, "but I don't much like the relationship between the bandage and the pillow." Indeed, they were stuck together. I went out to buy coffee and bagels, then we left for the post-op appointment. Dr. J. removed the bandage, checked Becky's eyes, and said everything looked perfect. She now had binocular vision! Her eyes were straight, she was using both at the same time, and had depth perception for the first time in her life.

We were four very excited people who made the two-hour drive home along the coast. Becky was wearing dark glasses since she wasn't supposed to be in too much light or over-use her eyes for a week. The girls both teased me that this was the first time ever that I hadn't told them to look for whales on this route.

It was a new world for Becky. She and I spent a good part of that first week sitting on the couch talking about what we could see. "Does the left side of the dresser look to you as if it's coming out into the room?" she asked. And, "I used to think walls were straight, but now they warp as I walk towards them." She said things looked round. "I don't know how I lived all those years in a flat world," she told me. It was so exciting to see her reach for something on the table and get it on the first try, or watch her look for the doorknob and put her hand right on it.

My Eye Surgery
Becky

My eyes were crossed for the first fourteen years of my life, so my only depth perception was what my brain could figure out from the relationship between things. There were tricks I picked up along the way. They all took time and figuring out. Part of what made math and numbers seem attractive to me was their reliability. Whenever you add two and two together you get the same answer: four. With my unreliable body it was a different story. My eyes are a good example of this. My brain would switch back and forth. Sometimes, it took information from one eye, sometimes the other. For instance, I might be reaching for something, then my mind would switch eyes. Everything would appear to have jumped around. My perspective had just made a sudden shift. I would end up not using my eyes that much.

When I was about 10 or 11, my dad took me and my adult-sized tricycle to a nearly deserted parking lot for me to practice riding. I was enjoying going fast, for the first time in my life! Then, I saw the side of a parked car. It was at the perimeter of the parking lot, not very close to me, but I didn't know that. I panicked and turned the wheel too quickly. Inertia took over my body and I went forward off the tricycle, ending up in the emergency room for stitches.

Ever since I can remember, my mom has done eye exercises with me. She would cover up one eye and ask me what I saw, then uncover it and cover the other eye and ask me the same thing. I remember my parents would arrange different cheeses and silverware or other small stuff on a cutting board in the kitchen and ask me which object was closer or further away. I got the right answers, and I figured my brain was fixing the dimensions. It was already accommodating for the fact that I was switching eyes by tilting my head. Also, I didn't rely on the information coming from my eyes. Since my eyes were crossed, I wasn't always looking at the same thing everyone else was. So, sometimes I would pretend to see something, then look later to see what it actually was.

I decided I wanted to have surgery on my eyes to straighten them. I thought I would be able to keep my head straighter and look at people and have them look back at me. We went to several specialists who said that the surgery could be done, but my eyes might go back to being crossed and so the surgery would have to be repeated.

Then I was referred to an optometrist who examined my eyes and said my vision was good in both eyes, but no amount of exercises could straighten them. She said that after the age of eight, the brain loses the ability to adapt to binocular vision. She referred us to someone in San Francisco who had developed a very successful technique of leaving a stitch in one eye and going back after the surgery to make sure the eyes were perfectly aligned.

We had a consultation with this surgeon, who examined my eyes and explained the surgery to me. On the car ride back home, my mom and I talked about all the things we liked about this doctor. We still didn't understand the binocular vision thing, but we figured I wouldn't have it because of the age eight thing. I decided to have the operation anyway for cosmetic reasons. We scheduled it for February. I wasn't supposed to read or go out much for a while after the operation. I remember our friends lending us books for my mom to read to me, but the only ones she read were what I needed for school.

Before the surgery, I wasn't consciously aware of being afraid of it, but I had dreams of going to school blind. Also, in art class that year we were asked to do a painting with different colors for different emotions. Mine was a self-portrait that people still comment on. It won a ribbon in the school art contest. My eyes are clearly crossed and my face is in shades of purple and blue.

Becky's Self-Portrait at 14

My grandmother, mother, sister and I went up the day before my surgery and got a motel room. I had a pre-op appointment with the surgeon. My mother said to the doctor, "I still don't understand why Becky won't have binocular vision after the surgery." He told her I would. This baffled us as to why we hadn't understood that after our first meeting with him.

The four of us were laughing and joking when we went out for Chinese food that night. The next morning, we all went to the hospital and my mother and grandmother said that I must be hungry and thirsty, because I wasn't supposed to eat or drink anything after midnight the night before. I remember Anna saying that she hadn't had anything to eat or drink yet that day either. I was always glad when some of the "poor Becky" attention got diverted. Anyway, I was too focused on the surgery to even know if I was hungry or thirsty, but I couldn't say that at the time.

That evening, when we were sent home, one of my eyes was still bandaged and I was out of it. The next day, the doctor took off the bandage. People seemed to float in and out of my field of vision. It was the weirdest thing.

Over the next few weeks, when I was recovering and still getting used to my new sight, I would describe to my mother what things looked like. I gained a literal understanding of how point of view changes. On the day that I went back to school, we had a substitute teacher for art class, and he told us to cover up one eye and draw our shoe. After I told him about my surgery, he said I could draw mine with both eyes open.

FOG Things
Dena

There are some things I don't like to say to Becky, but which I think I should, so that she is more "socially acceptable." I actually hate doing this. But who will if I don't? I've told her all this, and how if it were just the two of us living on an island somewhere, none of this would matter, but it's a fact that certain behaviors make your life easier when dealing with other people. So when I have something like this to say to Becky, I call it a FOG thing, For your Own Good. And we can joke about it, but neither one of us likes it. When I bring up a FOG thing, I can see her body tense, her smile suddenly fade. So I rarely do it.

However, Becky often chews with her mouth open. It's true that when she was a child, the best time to learn these things, I didn't fuss at her about it. I thought she had enough to deal with: holding the fork or spoon, not dropping the food, getting the glass to her mouth without spilling her drink, etc. Who cared if she didn't close her mouth while chewing? I certainly didn't. I probably didn't even notice. Instead, I cheered her on for what she *could* do.

But now that she's a teenager, it's embarrassing. To me, for her, when others are around. Of course I've told her about it, and suggested she watch to see how other people eat. I've shown her *Dear Abby* columns and other such things about how people don't like to see eaters chewing with their mouths open. But still she does it.

I don't want to ruin our mealtimes by pointing out FOG things, so I don't say anything while we're actually eating. Once I told her that I also would like to change my chewing habits; I wanted to do it more slowly. So we figured out a code that we could use to signal one another. It hasn't really worked for either of us.

Therapy Rant
Becky

My thoughts on the physical and speech therapy I received as a child are conflicted. On one hand, I feel I would have had a lot more problems in public school if I couldn't walk and talk at least as well as I did. The flip side is that, at times, I felt like whenever some new possibility of help became available, my parents were too quick to jump at it without seeing it in the context of the past things they had tried.

Sometimes it felt like I was an ongoing experiment. What would work? Everything came with some sort of promise of results. These promises were greater when the therapy was more expensive or extensive.

Speech therapy, for me, started in elementary school. At that time, the therapist would ask me questions about my day and tell me to avoid words with sounds that I was having trouble with. Later, I went to a private speech therapist who gave me a long list of things that I should do before speaking, such as make sure my vocal cords are ready, and told me not to avoid any sounds. The next therapist gave me relaxation techniques such as having me take a deep breath after sitting down and making sure that I was comfortable in the chair. This was another technique that was hard to replicate outside of the office. She gave me cards and told me to make up stories about the pictures. One "speech therapist" was actually a singing teacher. He had me reading from a magazine into a tape recorder while tapping myself. A friend of ours told us about a device called "SpeechEasy" that might enable me to speak smoothly. He didn't know that it amplified, slowed-down, and played back my voice and every other sound into my ear. One day my mother and I drove up to Petaluma to the lab where I tried this and my speech was clear but loud. It gave me a bad headache.

The last speech therapist that I went to tested me out on a newer version of this device and ordered one for me. She thought that I could use it in my everyday life, even though it had headphones and a thing attached to wires. When I told her about my previous experience, she said, "Well, maybe it's better now." The device is sitting in my "stuff" drawer unused. She also wanted me to get some sort of telephone adapter which I didn't get.

The summer before university, I met someone who remembered doing a Rolfing session (a kind of deep massage) with me as a child. When I told my dad of this encounter, he said, "Oh yeah, and you screamed in pain the whole time." My parents only took me once.

Feldenkrais bodywork did have some very significant and positive effects on my young body. Moshe Feldenkrais would do gentle range-of-motion exercises on me, showing my brain what my body could do. One time after an appointment, my eyes straightened for hours. After a few appointments, I put my hands out to catch myself in a fall for the first time in my life. One night, I dreamt that I had gone up the ladder and down the slide of our backyard swing set. The next morning, I got up and did just that. Another first!

I've had Feldenkrais work done on me by other therapists with varying results. Some people, like my dad, who studied with Feldenkrais and became certified, would pack too much into a session, and my body would be sore the next day. I knew that the sessions weren't supposed to hurt. Some therapists seemed to make a game out of it. After my very latest encounter with Feldenkrais bodywork, my center of gravity pushed back into place—undoing years of backpack wearing and using crutches.

I remember four different acupuncturists trying various things on me. The first two stuck incense-type things in my feet and lit them. The second one would stick a needle in my back and have me walk around for half an hour before she would take it out.

The third was in San Francisco and deserves her own story. The last one was someone I went to for Qigong, and he immediately started putting needles in my head, arms and legs. I think I felt better for about a day after most of these appointments.

Up until the age of 18 (when I put a stop to it), I went horseback riding once a week. This mid-week activity was great for my self-confidence. However, starting in third grade, I had to leave school early on Tuesdays, and didn't feel like doing homework afterwards. Being on a horse wore me out. And as well as my regular school homework, I also had homework for the ranch.

I'm glad I tried all of these different things, but in the long run I'm not sure if I can point to any one thing that helped me, or helps me, on a day-to-day basis. But maybe they all did. If I met parents of a baby with CP and they asked my opinion, I would tell them to try therapies that didn't hurt, but not to get their hopes up. Also, I found therapy on school days was often overwhelming; when my body was stressed with school it couldn't take on changes very easily. I'd tell these parents not to rely on one or even two kinds of therapy, but to do as much research as they can. And if there's one certain thing that's particularly important to them, or their child, or their family, then try and go to the source, or the inventor, or the top research facility, and get the help there. And I'd tell them their child might complain about the therapy, just as I do in this chapter.

An Acupuncture Appointment
Dena

I have mixed feelings about therapy for one's body. There's the question of *why*. Why do we put so much time, energy and money—not to mention pain—into various kinds of therapy? There is an implication that we're not accepting a person the way she is, and hence we devote enormous effort to changing that person so she appears more "normal." A woman using a wheelchair once told me she had had three surgeries on her foot when she was a child just so it would point straight ahead. "Why?" I asked. "My parents said it looked better," she told me.

I asked Becky once what she would do if she had a magic wand that could make any changes she wanted in her body. She thought for a moment and then told me she wasn't sure she'd choose not to have cerebral palsy.

"What if you could wave a magic wand and always be able to speak smoothly?" I asked.

"Well, yes," she said, "I'd do that."

"What if a magic wand would enable you to run?"

Long pause. "Well, yes. But, I don't think my mind would have worked the way it does if I hadn't had CP."

When she was seven, Becky told me, "At recess I wish I could walk and run and jump like the other kids. But it's nice like this too." She also told us, as a 7-year-old, "Sometimes your body tells you to do something and you can't do it, so you have to do something *similar* that you *can* do at that time."

So, by the time she was twelve, I had given a lot of thought to all the focus and attention that is put on a disabled child's body, or speech, as if these "faults" are the most important things about that person. What about the other aspects of a child's life? Becky had so much physical, speech, and occupational therapy in her young years that at this point she said she wanted to discontinue it all for a while. She'd been having weekly physical therapy sessions at a local hospital, speech therapy in school, horseback riding after school, and many kinds of nontraditional therapies such as acupuncture, acupressure, Rolfing, Reiki, Polarity, and several Feldenkrais sessions, including some with Moshe Feldenkrais himself. Fine, I said, let's forget it all and think about other things.

But then along comes someone else, waving something that just might be that magic wand, and I say, "Shall we try this?" And Becky says, "Sure." After a while it became something of a joke. So when we heard about an acupuncturist who had a reputation for doing amazing work on children and adults with brain damage, we made an appointment.

Walking into her office in the Phelan Building in San Francisco, where I used to go to my orthodontist a lifetime ago, I was disturbed by the way a small boy was screaming while having needles put into his scalp, and the way his mother was slapping him to try and stop his yelling. Becky and I looked at each other with silent questions, and then Becky asked me if I would be okay with this, since the last time I watched a doctor put a needle in her head, while stitching up a gash, I barely made it to the bathroom before throwing up.

When it was Becky's turn, Dr. L. told her it wouldn't hurt, and put seven needles in her head. I asked Becky how she was doing, and she said okay. The doctor then had her walk around the office. Dr. L.'s English was very poor and my Mandarin was nil, so communication was difficult. She wanted to know what "Becky's doctor" had said about her condition, so I tried to explain that Becky's brain damage was a birth injury, that she had been premature and had difficulty breathing at first.

Dr. L. watched Becky walk, then put two more needles in each ankle and had her take more steps, while touching her left leg a lot and saying, "Tight. Tight." She kept telling Becky to relax, but

Becky was becoming more and more frustrated. She told Becky the treatment wouldn't work if she didn't believe it in her heart, and by now Becky had tears in her eyes. I couldn't talk to this doctor because she didn't understand me, but I did tell Becky to be sure she knew that if this wasn't "working," *it wasn't her fault.*

After Dr. L. removed the needles and we left, Becky was crying, saying her head hurt. She asked me to see if any needles were still in her head. I looked, and gently felt around in her thick head of hair, and said no.

Many hours later, sometime after midnight, Becky came into my room holding a needle in her hand, and said, "Look what I just pulled out of my head."

Looking for a Needle in a Hair-Stack
Becky

My mother and I went up to San Francisco to see an acupuncturist who was highly recommended by someone who was always giving advice. We didn't know how much faith we should put into the person making the recommendation, but made the appointment anyway. Later, we realized this acupuncturist was one who many other people had been telling my mother about. Apparently, this visiting acupuncturist from China had gotten some very good results with young children. During the session, in broken English, she told us her success stories.

When we arrived at her office, she was sticking some needles into the head of a screaming boy. A woman sat next to him and hit him when he cried. She turned to us and said we needed to write our address, phone number, and my name and age on a sheet of paper. At that point, I thought she was Dr. L.'s assistant and translator who we were told might be there. Later we realized she was the boy's mother.

While we were witnessing this scene, I asked my mother if she would be okay with watching the acupuncturist put needles in my head. (I was thinking about a time when I had fallen and cut my head, and my mother had taken me to the hospital to get stitches. She had felt sick to her stomach and told me later that the sight of them stitching my head reminded her of seeing me for the first time, in an incubator, with a big needle in my head.) She assured me that she would be all right with the needles in my head now, and I told her that I felt okay about it too. While we were talking, the acupuncturist had finished putting the needles in the boy and started putting them in his mother. The boy's mother was acting perfectly calm while the needles were going in. My mother saw this and said to me, "Maybe that boy is screaming because he didn't like the *thought* of needles in his head."

Dr. L. had me sit on the edge of a massage table. She did some things with my legs and said they were tight. This fact was nothing new as I'd never been able to straighten either one of my legs. However, she repeated this over and over throughout the session as if it were a big discovery. I sat in a chair, and she unwrapped some needles and inserted them in my head. It hurt slightly as she put them in. I expected this and didn't say anything. She asked me to hold my breath and move my legs while she wiggled two needles in my legs. This also hurt a little bit, as was to be expected. She then put two needles in each ankle. These needles didn't hurt. Then, she made a phone call. When she was done, she asked me if my leg muscles had relaxed. When I told her that I couldn't feel any difference, she told me the reason her treatment wasn't working was because I didn't believe in it.

She then had me walk around both with and without my crutches. The needles hurt when I was walking. She rubbed something hard down my spine. I could hear it going down, and it didn't feel good. When I told her this, she did it to my mother who said it felt good to her. Then the acupuncturist took the garbage out. When she did this, my mother said that I seemed upset about something. I felt completely invalidated.

Because I wasn't relaxing, the acupuncturist told me to lie down. She pinched the skin together on my back all the way up to my shoulders. She then had me turn over. She did the same pinching on my stomach. While she did this, I told her one of the needles in my scalp was poking me, and that it hurt, but the acupuncturist didn't seem concerned. I thought I must have leaned against a needle. When she finally took the needles out, I didn't feel any relief. It continued to hurt where they had been.

When we left the building, I had a bad headache. I asked my mother to check and see if there were any needles still in my head. She said she felt one, but it was my ear she was touching. That made us giggle, but still no needles were found. Thinking I must have had a hunger headache, I said we should get something to eat. After we got our food, I started crying. When my mother asked me what the matter was, I told her that my head hurt. We talked about the session. We both said the things that we didn't like. Neither one of us could think of anything positive about Dr. L. During the whole evening, I kept touching my scalp to see if it was getting less sore. After we went home, I knew I wouldn't be able to sleep, so I read for a while. Before going to sleep, I felt my head again, and pulled out a needle.

An Oar in the Mainstream
Becky

I don't think growing up is easy for anybody, especially at the point when we are faced with the knowledge that there is a world outside of our family and friends. We have to explore life, and meet new people with different backgrounds and ways of living and being. For many people, this adjustment to other ways of living and being occurs during the first few years of schooling. After that, some people develop long-lasting or even life-long friendships.

My cerebral palsy has had its most severe effect on my walking, talking and writing. I didn't walk for the longest time, and even now, I use crutches for long distances or extra stability and speed. When I am under pressure, my speech often turns into a stutter, and this makes my talking slow and hard for the untrained ear or impatient person to understand. Handwriting is another activity that is slow and full of extra movements or jerks, which are magnified in my writing. Sometimes I take the time to change the especially bad pencil marks, but even then, it isn't perfect.

I was always different in my thinking and ways of doing things. I often did unusual activities for my age. When the other children were playing with jump ropes or running around, I would be sitting quietly just contentedly thinking, listening in on the older people talking. Talking and listening were ways to share my ideas, get some feedback, and hear new things to think about.

This was only the very beginning of my unusual enculturation, and is probably the main reason I have different values and ways of reacting to and interacting with other people. Peer pressure hardly ever reached me and even when it did, when I was young, I didn't much care what other people thought of me. Or so I liked to believe.

I think my elementary school years were typical for someone

who changed schools many times. I would transfer to another school when we'd move to a new district, or if my parents found a school that seemed better than the one I was going to. Sometimes I felt like I was skimming the surface of each individual school because I was never at the same one for more than two years. It seemed as if I was an oar being pulled out of one place and put into another. I also felt like I was an "or," meaning that I was an alternative—a student with a disability—for the teachers and administrators to think about and make accommodations for.

Being teased and feeling lonely were normal, I thought. This is true to a certain extent, but I based my thinking about it in an unhealthy way. I became extra-sensitive to teasing, and pretended that I liked being alone. I haven't quite gotten over these adaptations.

I am surprised now to think that I put up with face-to-face teasing for so many years. Did I accept it as a part of mainstreaming? In my mind, did I somehow think I deserved it? I could plainly see that no one else was being teased quite as much. The only explanation I can think of for having accepted such behavior is that it was the only thing I knew about.

No one should have to put up with other people intentionally making school life miserable for them. And I couldn't understand why students who were under the same pressures I was at school would want to take it out on a fellow student.

At the very beginning of high school, I considered joining two campus clubs, both of which sounded very intriguing. I thought the clubs would be a good way for me to meet new people with similar interests. But because my classes were so demanding, I didn't even try to join them. Wednesday was club day, so even if I had time that day, I would've had to choose between one club or the other.

Over the years, I've had trouble with some of my teachers, but I found I could usually solve these problems with a simple explanation or by getting to know them. In time I would prove myself, make them see our similarities and differences. One of the ways I did this was to speak up and answer questions in class. This would also make the other students aware of my willingness to be there and learn. They would realize that I was intelligent. I was in advanced classes in junior high and high school. Math has always been my strong subject.

I was a bright student with a disability. I cared about school. I went home and studied for hours. Other students made up their minds not to like me, and even to be against me. I knew it wasn't just me. High school is a bad experience for a lot of kids.

For me, school was problematic all the way through, not just high school. Sometimes I wondered if I was being hardened or softened by what was happening at school. Had I become insensitive, or taken too much to heart, unable to throw it off? I kept hoping it would get better, that the students would mature, and the school work would become more interesting, or at least that, maybe, I was making an impression on some of the teachers, if not the students. I have always expected not to fit in, but that doesn't make it any easier.

Some said high school was the time of their life. I don't know why the people I talked with before high school had such a good experience to tell and the people I talked to after my negative experiences had similarly bad stories to share. Did they want to get my hopes up and keep my expectations high? Personally, I would have preferred it if they had told me the way it really was so I would have been able to realistically prepare myself.

At school, I believe there is a mold for everyone to fit into, from the administrators to the teachers and students. If you fit into one of these molds, then you have friends and things are easy for you. But if you don't, they aren't.

One of my teachers once explained to me that things are taught in a spiral, and year after year they are supposed to touch on some of the same subjects, going deeper into them each time. That way, what students didn't understand the first time, they would get again the next year. My mind, personally, would shut off when I heard something that I already understood. So this style of teaching didn't work for me.

Questions in the Car
Dena

What? I said sharply
while driving down the freeway.
Out of the corner of my eye
I saw a sudden hard jerk
in Becky's body
as she sat in the passenger seat.

It was the *what* that means
What's going on?
Her sister used to say it as a child
when she'd see a certain look
on my face: *Mommy, what?*

Now I wanted to know
what was happening with Becky.
Did she have a pain?
Was she okay?

I was changing my position
she said evenly.
Does that require
an explanation?

A couple of miles down the road
I looked over at her and said
You know, you could ignore
a lot of my questions.

Pushing Me On
Becky

At the school meeting before ninth grade, my math teacher announces he can't give me extra time for in-class tests. He refuses to change the way he teaches. My mother tells him that it is the law, and he has to make reasonable accommodations. He doesn't care. He's *not* going to change. I groan in silence, knowing that he is the only one who teaches advanced honors algebra. All the other teachers at the meeting say they are okay about having me in their classes.

I am the only one who comes here on a special bus for disabled students. When we stop at a red light, the driver leans on her horn until the light changes. When a certain commercial comes on the radio, she'll sing along. Sometimes, the bus is late getting me to school. This becomes a point of contention between me and my first-period teachers. When my mother and I tell the bus driver that I need to be at school on time, she complains about our streets being too narrow.

I try to start a club for students with disabilities. I have an idea for a disability awareness day. Some of my teachers think it's a good idea too. I put out a call on the daily announcements for interested students to meet in a certain classroom. While the announcement is being read, I hear sneers from the students around me, like, "Who would want to go to *that?*" I keep my mouth closed. I am the only person who shows up at the meeting. This is the one wheelchair-accessible high school in the county. I know I'm not the only student with a disability. If I were, I wouldn't have even tried to start a club.

My problems with the other students intensify this year. When I drive my scooter through the halls, I hear "Missed" from someone who has thrown something in my direction. One day, as

I sit on the grass to eat lunch, there are students on the roof of the building throwing gummy bears at me. I get up and leave.

One such lunch time, I go into my academic counselor's office. She gets me all excited about a biology class that focuses on ecology. Three biology teachers will co-teach it. I come home feeling something good is coming out of my loneliness, and I share this excitement with my mother.

Many things go wrong with the biology class. One teacher has a habit of asking math questions (e.g., What is the name for one followed by a hundred zeros?). I am often the only student who knows the answer, or at least the only one who raises her hand. Because I raise my hand so frequently, the teachers ask the principal to tell me not to ask questions in class. My speech is too slow and takes up class time. If I have something to say, I should wait until lunch time. (This sets many things in motion, including the addition of speech therapy to horseback riding as another weekly extra-curricular activity for me.) The principal tells this to the aide who works with me, and the aide tells me. I am furious about this because I don't get a lunch break anyway. When the teachers "lose" two of my weekly assignments and give me an "F" for the first half of the semester, that is the final straw.

I switch to a different biology class taught by the only other biology teacher at the school. After I change classes, the two papers are found. The new class works out just fine. When the teacher announces that she's not going to teach biology next year, I am stuck. In order to graduate, I would need to take another biology class next year. What am I going to do? I don't feel like taking one of the other teachers' classes, but they are the only ones who will be teaching it.

While all this biology stuff is going on, I am having problems with other teachers as well. My Spanish teacher wants us to work in groups. One day, she hands out a worksheet and tells us to get into groups of two or three. I start out by asking the people who are sitting by themselves. They say they want to do the assignment alone. Then, I ask people already in groups and they say no. When I tell the teacher this, she announces to the class: Becky doesn't have a partner—does anyone want her in your group? The whole class goes completely silent. This incident prompts the Resource Specialist to go into all of my classes and give talks about disability awareness.

My first-period class is California history. We discuss Mexican history, the Native Americans, and the early explorers. I like the slant in this class. One day, the bus makes me late and the teacher comes to the door and literally pushes me out of the classroom saying that he is giving a surprise quiz, and I can't come in because I am late.

I like to think that he and the other teachers pushed me all the way to Cabrillo Community College. I left high school after the tenth grade.

Decision
Dena

The lunchtime crowd had left, and it was too early for dinner, so we were the only ones on the restaurant's patio overlooking the creek. It had been my idea to come here. I needed a drink. As I sat with my hand around my glass, Becky looked straight into my eyes and told me, in that serious way she has, that she was quitting school.

"I can't do this anymore," she said. We had just come from a meeting at her high school, and I can't remember now if it was the meeting I called because her biology teacher told her not to ask questions in class because her speech was too slow, or the meeting I called when her history teacher pushed her back out of the classroom after the special bus dropped her off late, or the meeting that was set up because her Spanish teacher had said to the class, "No one picked Becky for their group, so who will take her?" and no one had answered.

"I'm tired of being the trailblazer," she told me, her brown eyes wide and sad. Her word for herself made me think back to the time ten years earlier when I had watched her go eagerly into her first-grade classroom, her walker drawing curious looks from the other children. She was filled with excitement and expectation, and the innocence of a six-year-old.

"Okay," I said, knowing what she had been through in her first two years of high school. That is, I thought I knew. It would be years before I found out things that neither Becky nor Anna told me at the time. "What do you want to do, then?"

"I want to take the high school equivalency test and go to Cabrillo," she said. "You can do that when you're sixteen."

I looked at her, and imagined her going to our local community college. I smiled.

"Let's drink to that," I said, and clinked my margarita against her lemonade.

Riding Free
Becky

The first time I was on the back of a Peruvian Paso horse, as a Dragon Slayer at Rivers' Crest Stables, I felt as if I were running with, instead of on, the horse. The horse was doing the Paso gait, which is a fast walk named after the Peruvian Paso breed, and not as bumpy as a gallop. Because of my CP, and walking with crutches, running has always fascinated me. I fantasize about how it must feel, the way some people might try to imagine flying. On Tierra del Fuego, the mare I was riding at the time, my whole body was bouncing or moving: my legs were going away from the horse, my upper body was bouncing up and down, and my hands were going all about. At the same time, I had the feeling of smooth movement through space with an ease and comfort that I imagine as part of running.

Rivers' Crest Riding Stables gives free riding lessons to anyone in our community who has a disability and is willing to slay the dragon from within. I originally became a Dragon Slayer as a form of physical therapy. Horseback riding stretches and exercises the body as well as building self-confidence. The self-esteem and satisfaction that come from looking back and realizing all you've done aren't simply by-products, but are some of the goals of the Dragon Slayers program.

When I started out in the program as a nine-year-old, I groomed the horses and studied their anatomy and the names and functions of different parts of the saddle.

At seventeen, I now ride in and around the Forest of Nisene Marks State Park. It is very beautiful and soothing to ride on a trail in the woods. I regularly ride on two different trails. One is short and lined with overhanging redwood trees. The other trail, a longer ride, passes an open uphill area, then goes under a tree that has fallen over a narrow part of the trail. This leads to a clearing at the intersection of five more trails. Sometimes, I can hear a nearby creek.

A big earthquake last October seems to have had an effect on everything. I grew up thinking of my body as being unstable and the rest of the world as very solid, but after the earthquake I found I had to revise this view. One result of this 1989 quake, whose epicenter was right there in the park, was that the road leading into the park and the stables was closed for a month. When I was able to resume horseback riding, the horse I was on sensed that my body was a little tense and slightly off-balance. On that particular day, walking was hard enough (as happens to me sometimes), not to mention horseback riding. My trainer wanted the horse and me to go quickly into the Paso gait, which takes a lot of balancing on my part, and I didn't feel comfortable doing it. Despite my hesitancy, I would have done it if the horse hadn't refused to move. She must have known by the way I was sitting that I wasn't up to the bounce and jostle of the Paso gait.

I usually ride in a Western saddle, but over the years I have had other riding experiences. I've tried riding bareback, which has been difficult, since sitting straight on a moving horse is almost impossible for me, even with the security of a saddle. My body has ached from trying to sit up with the horse's spine poking in my crotch. Also, I've tried riding on an Eastern saddle, which is less secure than a Western one. This was difficult because whenever the horse turned, or put her head down, or jumped, I almost fell off her. We adjusted the stirrups to try to alleviate the problems, but it was a frustrating experience. Every time the stirrups were adjusted, my sense of balance and leverage on the horse's head changed, too. It was challenging having many things at once altered from what I was used to.

Over the years, I've come to understand the personalities of the horses I ride, and I can tell by looking at their ears or the way they turn their heads when they are thinking of stopping or turning to eat. I feel a connection with the horses that goes a lot deeper than just the reins that I hold in my hands.

I sometimes push myself to do things I don't feel up to doing in order to prove that I can do them. I challenge myself up to and even past my limit; this limit is my dragon. I've welcomed this challenge into other aspects of my life, too.

Reality Check
Dena

Talking about the day, drinking iced tea
in fancy glasses
we watch the ducks, laugh about next week
when so much company is coming

We stand, stretch, it's time to go in
"I'll take the glasses," she says
I sit back down
"Becky, why do you always say that
when I can so easily do it?"

I have visions of her falling
Her body cut with shattered glass
It's the same with scissors, knives, pencils
"Is it that you want to prove you can?"

She walks away, empty-handed, head down
Then turns to look at me, straight-on, serious
"The thing is, you see, I never think of falling."

A Clean Break
Becky

When I went to Cabrillo, I found a whole different world than grade school. I could pick my classes. They were only two or three days a week. There was a computer lab close to the classes which any student could go into. I could study what I wanted. This was my first time experiencing an office devoted to supporting students with disabilities. One of the people in that office had been a friend all my life. I would go in there a lot. I quickly became friends with the other people who worked in the Disabled Students Programs and Services Office. They had their own academic counselor, who I found out later used to live in the redwoods near my grandmother.

In the summer after I left high school, while I was taking some placement tests, I also attended an adaptive swimming class at Cabrillo. The person teaching the class had also taught my high school adaptive PE class, so she knew me, and invited me to come to the adaptive workout room before swimming. These two classes were surprising to me. Instead of me having to fit my body into the class, the classes fit themselves around the students' individual bodies. Cabrillo continued to impress me for a total of three years.

In my first semester, my mother and grandmother went with me to an awards ceremony where I was receiving a scholarship for the next semester. After it was over, my mother commented on how many people came up to me and we started talking about this or that. This made me aware that I'd made a few friends and that I really did fit in to all aspects of college.

A year after I started going to Cabrillo, Anna realized how happy I was there, and took the equivalency test too. She took two years to transfer to a university, whereas I took three.

In my last semester at Cabrillo, I took a weekend Mother-

Daughter class. There, I discovered how unique the relationship between my mother, my sister Anna, and me really was. We could laugh and joke about our misunderstandings. This prevented them from becoming any big deal. I feel this has had a very positive impact on our relationship. Humor is one thing that we have a lot of in our family. Not only is it a good way to release any built-up tension and express feelings of dissatisfaction, but I feel it is an indicator of how strong and unconditional the bond between us is.

A woman at the weekend class got up and told of a tradition of giving a high school graduate a chest to put childhood possessions in. She went on to say how important a ceremony is for a graduate, or when someone gets married and moves out of the house. Meanwhile, my sister, my mother, and I were thinking that Anna and I weren't going to go through any of these acknowledged ways of separation.

We all realized the importance of a ceremony to recognize that a phase of our lives would soon be over. Because Anna and I both left high school early, neither of us went through the high school graduation ceremony.

After listening to the story of the graduation chest, I began thinking we should do something to mark our pending transition. My mother and Anna and I came up with a ceremony that would honor all of our upcoming changes.

We decided we would talk about our feelings about the future. Also, the three of us would honor how good our lives were together. There is no doubt that we'd discuss our apprehensions about the future. But along with doing this we'd be excited for each other. We would all be going through many changes. This ceremony would help ease our fears about that change. We planned to use hand-made candles and involve water in our ceremony. Anna and I had grown up near the ocean and the use of water in the ceremony symbolized us. Also water flows seamlessly from one thing to the next, so it seemed like a good medium to involve in a transition ceremony.

Leaving Home
Dena

It was a great change for Becky when she went to Cabrillo College. The students were there because they wanted to be, and the teachers were sensitive and enthusiastic. Also, there were other students with disabilities, and a very supportive and active office for disabled students.

Anna, following Becky's lead, also left high school at 16 and went to the community college. Although Anna started a year later, Becky took fewer classes each semester, so they were ready to transfer to the University of California at the same time: Becky to Santa Cruz and Anna to Berkeley. We were all a little anxious about this transition, and talked a lot about where they might live, what classes they should take, and what it might be like living on their own. They were both excited and apprehensive about leaving home, and I was sad to see them go.

One night as we sat around our dining-room table trying to fit their whole lives into the narrow lines of their university applications, I was acutely aware that this was both the beginning and the end of something. I sorted through my memories for the years when Anna was a camp counselor and when Becky won the math contests, and tried to imagine what it would be like at the table without them.

We went to Berkeley one weekend to look for a place for Anna to live. On Saturday we saw several possibilities, and as we were approaching the Bay Bridge to go to San Francisco where we were spending the night with a friend, Becky said she felt sick. I couldn't stop anywhere as we were caught in the bridge traffic, so I told her to roll her window down and get some fresh air. But there was no stopping her nausea, and minutes before we reached the toll plaza she threw up all over herself and the car. Anna, sitting in the back, grabbed the piece of material I kept over the back seat to cover the rips in the upholstery, and tried to help Becky clean up. She was quite a sight there in the passenger seat, and we've often wondered what the woman in the tollbooth thought.

When we reached our friend's apartment, Anna and I helped Becky, drenched with vomit, out of the car, drawing some rather puzzled looks from passersby. We helped her get undressed and into a bath, and tried to figure out what in the world had caused this. Nothing else seemed to be wrong, and we had all eaten the same food. We thought maybe it was the realization that Anna was moving out of Becky's life in a very big way, and that she too would be leaving Anna and me.

Becky had a plan for moving out on her own. The first year she was going to live in a student apartment on campus, and the second year she'd live in town with other students. This was the same town where I lived, but she wanted to live apart from me, to see how she would manage. A friend of mine once said to me, "Of course, Becky will always live with you." I was stunned by this comment, as I often am by things people say about Becky.

Anyway, off Becky went, excited and confident, to live in an apartment with four other girls on the campus of UC Santa Cruz. It pains me deeply when I think of what happened to her there. At the beginning, it seemed fine. But by the end of the school year she was crushed and defeated. I had never before seen her that way.

When I look back on this time, I wonder if some of the problems could have been prevented. Perhaps some kind of disability awareness might have been organized with her housemates.

Becky was a junior, transferring from a community college; the other students were in their first year. Two of the young women were old friends with each other from southern California and shared one of the bedrooms. The other two shared a second bedroom, and Becky had a room to herself, closest to the bathroom. It was a ground-floor accessible apartment.

Little by little, things started to go wrong. I had to pry information out of Becky. She wouldn't let me know of any problems, but I could hear in her voice that she was troubled. Her housemates would put her kitchen things in cabinets too high for her to reach. They stopped talking to her. Becky said she tried to call meetings to talk things over, but the others didn't want to participate.

Was my friend right? Would Becky always live with me?

You might think Becky would break a lot of things, but she doesn't. The only thing she broke when living with her roommates that first semester was her own teapot lid. Once she let her wok get too hot while she was preparing vegetables to stir-fry, and when she put it in the sink and turned the water on it, the wok melted a spot on the rubber dishpan and some of the water splashed onto one of the housemate's arms and burned her. The burn was not serious, and later that day Becky took the bus downtown to buy a new dishpan.

But her housemates turned against her, began to blame her for things that weren't right, ignored her, and eventually complained to the preceptors that she was dangerous to live with.

Thus began a series of meetings between Becky and the preceptors, with Becky becoming more and more sad and disheartened. Much of what was happening I didn't know about at the time, but my heart was breaking to see the state she was in. This was a person who, when she lived at home, was full of cheer and always ready to lend a hand to any task. She gave unselfishly of herself and her things, cared deeply about other people, and laughed and giggled at jokes and absurdities.

One day, full of despair, in the kitchen of her apartment, she took a plastic bag and started to put it over her head. A housemate ran to the preceptor, and this eventually led to Becky being asked to leave. Because of student confidentiality, I didn't know of the bag incident until later. Becky had always wanted to handle things herself, so she attended various meetings with university staff with no advocate present for her. Where was the Disabled Resource Center staff? Where was I? Why didn't Becky ask for an advocate? The whole thing was a mess.

When I talked to Becky later, she said she never intended to try and kill herself with the plastic bag; she only wanted to do something dramatic to let her housemates know how bad she was feeling. The university staff said her housemates didn't want to live with her anymore, and if she didn't leave, they would. A single dorm room was offered to Becky for the rest of the year, but she insisted on another apartment with housemates.

Becky and I, as well as Anna, who was home for the holidays, had many talks about all this. I wanted to throw my arms around Becky, bring her back home, and not let anyone hurt her. But I didn't say it quite like that. "You can always move back home," I told her. Anna, on the other hand, told Becky in no uncertain terms that she should *not* move back home, that it would mean defeat, that she should find somewhere else to live.

By the time Becky was due to return to school, the university had offered her another apartment with two women on another part of the campus. For the rest of the school year Becky lived with these housemates without any problems. She seemed, even, to be having a good time.

What was the difference in these two living arrangements? Had Becky learned something about living with others? About asking for help? Were the second women more mature, more sure of themselves? What happened to lead the first group to turn into a *Lord of the Flies* sort of situation, with Becky the scapegoat for all that went wrong? Indeed, the two groups of women were different. The first roommates were young, away from home for the first time, conservative in attitude. The second ones had more experience in the ways of the world, seemed more radical in appearance and behavior. "I love it," Becky said of the one whose punk hair was purple, "she doesn't care what anyone thinks."

So that was Becky's first year of living away from home. The second year, as was her plan, she lived with other students in rented houses in town. I hinted that she might want to continue living with the two women since it was working out so well, but Becky was firm in wanting to live off campus. She lived in two different places, with men and women, good times and not so good, probably a typical student's experience.

Meanwhile, things were not going well at school. Becky was having problems communicating with the teachers. She felt discouraged and talked of quitting. She cried easily and said she felt as if the whole school was against her.

"Going down the road feeling bad," sang the Grateful Dead on the radio as I drove home from work one day. The knot in my stomach tightened as I thought about the meeting that morning on UCSC's decision to bar Becky from attending. The meeting was with five staff members from the university. They said there had been behavior issues (because Becky got angry on a bus) and class-room problems (poor communication with teachers). I saw a staff person (from the Disability Resource Center, no less) ignore Becky's statement that the bus was late. "They're never late," she told Becky in the meeting. "Wait a minute," I said, "Becky just told you it *was* late!" Becky said this sort of thing happens all the time. Only one staff person at that meeting, the head of the Computer Board, saw things differently. While others complained about Becky's progress in some of her classes, and with Becky trying to explain some of the difficulties she had communicating with certain professors and some of the problems she'd had with the computers, he looked at Becky's record and said that she had successfully passed some very difficult courses, and obviously didn't need a tutor, as some at the meeting were suggesting, but perhaps, instead, she could use an advocate.

Ultimately, Becky was allowed to continue, on probation,

without an advocate, and did fine. I think in the process she learned a bit more about being her own advocate, but what a long hard road she traveled to find this strength.

Poison Oakes
Becky

All through my school experiences, my mother had told me things would get better later in my school career. When I was in grade school, the next school would be better. In junior high, my lot was going to improve once I got to high school. In high school, I thought that once I got to college, people would not care that I have a disability, that ideas would be the important things. Before Cabrillo, I wasn't at any one school for more than two years. Every time I went to a new school, I thought of it as an opportunity for a new beginning. My parents usually had to put up a fight to get my sister and me into these different schools. They did it because they thought it would be better for me, and I couldn't help but catch their optimism. As much as they wanted a particular school to be a positive experience, I wanted it even more.

No one realized the patterns until I got to university, but each time I started a new school, the same things would always happen. First, the other students wouldn't talk to me, but because I was the new kid, I expected this. Then the trouble would begin. In my early years the school staff was, for the most part, on my side. When the other students would tease me excessively, I would tell one of my teachers. A little bit of teasing didn't cause me to worry. I was different and people were afraid of difference. My mother told me that these students were immature. I would see, she said, that once I got older these problems would disappear. The fact that my teachers seemed to understand backed up this immaturity theory.

When I was still in high school, the person in charge of special admissions and some other school officials at the University of California at Santa Cruz met with my mother. Afterwards, when my mother told me about the meeting, UCSC sounded like the right place for me. From this meeting, we found out that three university classes were considered a full load. I was taking five at the time in high school. The average university student took five or six years to get a degree. All these things combined to comfort me and give me the impression that things would be easier in college.

However, because I left high school early—I was really an eleventh grader and only 17—I didn't think I was ready to go to UCSC. I knew of other students my age who were taking or had taken classes at Cabrillo Community College. I gave Cabrillo a try and had some of my best school years there. Everyone at Cabrillo seemed happy to be attending and to learn new things. The students and teachers showed an interest in my thought processes, and I was interested in theirs. My troubles with teasing and taunting disappeared at Cabrillo. Then, when I was ready to transfer to university, I went to UCSC.

UCSC has an extremely spread-out and very hilly campus. It is so spread out that there are shuttle routes and a city bus to take students from one part of campus to another. The Disabled Resource Center runs its own van. The campus is set in the trees. Once, I walked right past a building two or three times before I got a glimpse of it through the trees. Most of the buildings are in clusters called colleges. I was at Oakes College. UCSC offers dorms and apartments on campus. Each college has some on-campus housing as well as classrooms.

UCSC differed from Cabrillo in so many ways, and there were many things I didn't know about university life. Strangely, at UCSC I felt as if I were back in high school. The other students seemed shallow. They wouldn't even say "hi" to me. After class, everyone was in such a hurry that they didn't stick around to talk. People would also get to the classroom just in time for class. This made it hard to meet people. The only chances to meet were in class or where you lived.

As well as having these problems making friends, I had trouble with my professors and the Disabled Resource Center. It was 1992 and I was twenty years old. One of my classes was in computer graphics. We had to do all the work in a certain computer lab on campus. This lab had only regular computer mice that the students had to use. At the time, I didn't have enough coordination in my hands to use a regular mouse; I could only use a TrackBall mouse. I asked for a different mouse or a different computer, but ran up against a brick wall. No one, not even the DRC office, would do anything.

In addition, my housemates, who I thought were my friends, turned against me. They began to make up things that I had done and go en masse to the preceptor in charge of the building. One housemate rearranged the kitchen and put my stuff on a shelf that was out of my reach. Things weren't going so well, and I thought it would be good to meet periodically, so I tried to get the household to have regular meetings. I thought this would defuse the problems before they became major issues, so I proposed that we have dinner together once a week. I thought it would be nice if we all took turns cooking for these meals. All four of them refused. They said that they didn't have to check in with anyone anymore.

There was one housemate that I was particularly friendly with. We would have involved conversations. She would tell me about the customs of her native India. I let her and her friend use my computer for their papers. Another one of the housemates owned the phone in the apartment. There were some problems with the phone that they always blamed on me. After things started getting bad, I said that no one could use my computer, which was in my bedroom. One night not long after this, the telephone was taken into its owner's bedroom. I asked if I could use it, and was told that I couldn't. It was now my turn to go to the preceptor and complain.

I re-examined my whole life to try to figure out why every aspect of it seemed to be going so badly. Things hadn't worked out the way I had planned. I suddenly saw my school experiences not as isolated incidents but as a continuum that was getting worse. I felt awful. I was angry at the world. I would go around the apartment crying. I couldn't handle it, and I wasn't taking care of myself. One evening, I put a plastic bag over my head. I don't know what got into me. I wasn't thinking of dying.

The housemate in the next room shouted something like, "Get that thing off." I did. She went to tell the other housemates what had happened. All of us went up to the preceptors' office together. By this time, the preceptors already had a very bad image of me. We sat around as a group and talked about the household. I didn't hear too much at this meeting. I was dealing with the fact that I had just put a plastic bag over my head and what that meant.

Later, a meeting was set up with the provost and me. I had an idea that the provost wanted to throw me out of Oakes. An old family friend, who had been a professor at Oakes, sent an email message to the provost, saying that I was a good friend of hers and that she had talked me into living at Oakes. So the provost canceled the meeting and set up another one. My mother offered to come with me, but I told her I'd be okay by myself. I didn't think there was any need for anyone else. I went alone to the meeting, and there were two other people from the Oakes administration besides the provost. They made me sign a document saying that I wouldn't have any more emotional flare-ups. If I did, they would kick me out of Oakes.

I didn't tell any of this to my mother. One evening, I called her and told her I was thinking of taking some time off from school. I felt I needed a complete change of scene. I thought I might do some traveling. She talked me out of quitting school. "You have so much to lose by quitting now," she said. "Also, it won't be much longer."

Some of the UCSC computer labs are open 24 hours. One night, I went to finish an assignment. When I left the lab in the morning, I thought I would get off schedule if I went and slept.

However, not sleeping made me even more tired when I finally went to bed. The people in the apartment above were having an authorized party. The noise was unbelievable, but I couldn't complain because the party had been approved by Oakes. I was furious. The next morning, I turned my radio up loud. It felt good at the time. That afternoon when my mother came to pick me up, the preceptor was there to tell her that they were probably going to throw me out of Oakes for turning up the radio. My mother and I had a tearful car ride up the coast to my aunt's birthday dinner. When we got there, I didn't feel like celebrating, so I went to sleep.

Later that month, my mother and I had a meeting with the Disabled Resource Center staff. At that meeting, they made it sound as if they were there to help. All I had to do was ask. Earlier, I had gone in to tell them about some stairs that didn't have a banister. The woman I spoke to was my service coordinator at the time. When I went in, I noticed a poster on her door that said to notify her if there were barriers that needed to be removed to accommodate wheelchair users. The response I got about the banisters was, "What do you expect us to do about it?"

School officials acted differently when my mother was with me at meetings. This fact left me disgusted and frustrated. Why were they only mean when I was by myself? I began to think that my mother had a positive view of these people. This made me feel even more alone. My way of dealing with this was to go to the meetings by myself. I felt this was the only way to get the truth out of these people. Also, I wanted to know that I could take care of everything on my own. I didn't plan on staying in Santa Cruz my whole life. I was using UCSC as a training ground for me to be independent.

One night, before another meeting with the DRC, my aunt, uncle, sister, mother and I talked about what I should do. My aunt told of being in college at eighteen and really wanting to go home. My uncle said that he felt a lot of stress on him at college. My sister didn't think it was a good idea for me to move home. My mother did, because it would be easier. I didn't know what to think.

I decided to stay, and the DRC office found me an apartment at Kresge College. Kresge had been my first choice after walking around on campus before enrolling. The DRC office had recommended Oakes for me; I still don't know why. Kresge was the closest to most of my classes and had a reputation for being a feminist college. I really enjoyed being at Kresge. My two new housemates and I would talk about computers. One of them had originally been a computer major, and the other one had taken a computer-for-physics-majors class taught by the same person I had taken a C programming class from. We had a mutual disliking for his teaching style. There was a freer atmosphere in this house. I got to meet more people. There was a store within walking distance.

All in all, I feel that the problems with the professors and the administration were par for the course and something that I just had to deal with and get through, but I definitely could have handled everything else better. I had a lot of growing up to do.

Becky vs. the University

Dena

It seems she lost her cool
on a very rainy day
Grabbed a clipboard in the van
which had been late every time
Said she wanted to read the schedule

They say she violated a code of conduct
Threw her crutches, shouted too
She denies it, says she fell in the van
There was a meeting, four of them & Becky
She says they did not let her have her say

I have dreams of her being trampled
And blown up
Neither can I nor do I do enough
Only yell assorted directions
I cannot see in these dreams if she's okay

In the morning she falls, scrapes her neck
Cries, then stops, says she's okay
My tears don't stop but don't show either

I kiss her goodbye, she promises to call
after she's looked at the papers
the Disabled Resource Center says she must sign
before she's allowed
to ride their van again

She does not want me to intervene
Says it makes a stronger statement
if she handles it herself

I can't do anything if she won't let me
And anyway, I won't be here forever

The Meetings
Becky

To my mother

I called
to tell you
I was thinking of dropping out.

You dissuaded me, saying
I have so much invested in
my education.
It would be a waste
to quit now.
I thought about your words
and the years and hours
you spent at meetings
so I'd be allowed in.
You were right, it all would've been wasted.

But there are problems.
No one listens to what I have to say.
I am barred from the university.

Later, when we are talking,
you see the hurt that I was calling from.
We discuss my future.
Is it worth struggling for re-admission?

Meetings were set up.
I was invalidated twice
by the person whose job
is to support disabled students.

You can hardly believe that.

Are Things Any Better?

Dena

"Look at this article in the paper," I said to Becky one day when she was home for a visit. "It's about a gay comedian. He went to your high school, and says the kids used to throw fruit at him. He says no one—not a teacher, a counselor, a friend, or the principal—ever helped him."

Becky looked at me for a minute before saying anything. "They used to throw things at me when I was on my scooter," she said. "And at lunch time when I was sitting eating they'd throw food at me."

I stood there with my mouth open, as I often did at things she told me long after they had happened.

"Did you tell anyone? Did anyone try to stop it?"

"I don't remember," she said, and went into her room to finish getting ready to go back to her apartment.

Sometime later I asked her, "Would UCSC students throw food at you?"

"No"

"See! Things *are* better now that you're older." I was hoping this thing I'd been saying to her all her life was finally coming true.

"I'd rather they throw food than put my food things so high I can't reach them. It's just different."

Whose Community?
Becky

I belong to the community that my mother has built around herself and her two daughters. It is made up of close friends and family. It consists of some people my mother has known as far back as her own childhood, but there is no distinction in closeness between the ones she grew up with and those she met later. When I'm among this group of people, it doesn't matter that my sister and I are the youngest, meaning that we have the least life experience. We participate fully in all discussions.

Because my mother went to college in Oregon, she still has friends who live there. It is like a reunion when we take a trip up north. For years, my mother would make a point of going to Oregon about every other year and visiting with these old friends. My sister and I would usually join her on these summer excursions.

Part of why I think of these friends from out of state as being in the same community as those in my home town is because I get the same feeling of inclusion from being around them. There is a certain indescribable lightness that usually comes over me. This feeling comes only from being around people who know me well enough not to care how different I am. In fact the people in this community value each other precisely for their differences.

These are, after all, the friends to whom we have gone for support. It gives me a warm feeling to know there are people who are so close to me that they'll be there to back me up no matter what happens.

It was one of these good friends who turned out to be my only advocate when I was having trouble with the university. No one from any of the Student Services offices was on the side of a new student with a disability who was being asked to leave by her college.

It is because of this experience at UCSC that I worry about moving away. Occasionally, I think, what if I hadn't had the support of friends who just so happened to have an "in" at the university? How would I deal with a future situation of not being listened to? Where would I turn if no one believed me? What if something that I wasn't able to handle on my own popped up again? How would I deal with it? Without friends like these, I would be lost. These are all concerns for which I have to find the answers within myself before I can be okay about leaving. The ironic thing, though, is that it is from the same people who make it hard for me to go that I get the feeling that I have to break away.

I guess the fact that I do have these ambivalent feelings about moving away shows the connection that I have with the people here. However, I know that in this society, this change is going to have to happen. Somehow, I think it would be so easy to live here my whole life, but that would be like saying I didn't want to grow up.

One of the reasons that I feel so connected to many of these people is because of the equality when we're together. It doesn't matter that I take longer to get my words out, or slow everyone else down when we all go for a walk. These friends have shown me over and over again that they are willing to wait so I can be included in the group activities.

Now, I realize I was expecting this same treatment when I went to school and met new people. I soon found, to my disappointment, that most people weren't like that. Because I was different from them, my classmates couldn't relate to me. Because I saw their inabilities to accept me, I didn't want to count myself as one of them. This caused me to feel stuck as far as friendships were concerned. Throughout my schooling, for the most part, I've been closer to my teachers than my peers. This is why community is a loaded word for me. The people whom I can say anything to aren't like me. On the other hand, those whom I have the most in common with won't have anything to do with me.

Quality of Life
Dena

I've asked Becky many times and in many ways if she's happy with her life. (I know I'm obsessed with this!) She always thinks a while, and answers yes. Once I asked her if she was: (a) very dissatisfied, (b) somewhat dissatisfied, (c) felt life was just okay, (d) that it was generally pretty good, or (e) that it was always very good. She smiled and said she thought her life was generally very good.

Another time I asked her to rate her quality of life on a scale of one to ten. After thinking about it, she said nine. Before going to UCSC, she said, it was a 10.

Does she say these things just to make me feel good? I don't think so. She's stunningly honest. When asked a question, she'll give a carefully considered answer, sometimes taking the questioner by surprise. And she is by nature a cheerful person. As a child she always woke up eager to greet the day, happy and in a good mood. Once when the girls were little, the three of us were playing cards with my dad. He shuffled the cards in an unusual way and said, "This is a new kind of shuffle." When it was Becky's turn to shuffle, she accidentally scattered the cards all over the table, then said, "This is a Becky kind of shuffle."

And even now, at 23, she nearly always wakes up with a smile. Her problems, she says, come from other people's attitudes. *She* is happy with herself. *They* are uncomfortable, and it is manifested in evasion, condescending behavior, meanness, and putting up barriers of various kinds. This is what makes her life difficult.

The Laughing Cousin
Becky

There is a picture of the three female cousins by the river.
They are holding on to each other, & me clearly happy.
I have both hands in my lap and on my face is a full-fledged laugh.
We have all had our hard times.

Unfortunately, Anna's bad times
were because of her being my sister.
She stood up for me to other school kids,
then had some of the same teachers.
At home, she justifiably felt ignored.

Our cousin had her own health issues
and then growing-up problems.

At the time, I thought most of my problems
were with the world beyond.
People's actions and attitudes didn't always add up
to their words of inclusion.

So when I was home, I was comfortable being myself.

Perspective
Becky

When I was twenty-one, my mother and I were sitting around with a disability rights activist whom I had just recently met. She was saying how my parents had done me a great disservice by not getting me involved with the disability community. I'm not sure I would have wanted someone to tell me what barriers lay ahead. I was happy in my own world where tomorrow held a promise and yesterday didn't matter anymore.

At the time, I thought my parents and other family members and friends did the opposite for me. They made sure that I was comfortable associating with anybody and everybody. The majority of the people I will to have to deal with in my life won't have a disability.

I might have changed my whole life around on the advice of disability activists. I don't know how that would've been. As I'm writing this, I'm thinking about what the 23-year-old Becky would have to say to an earlier self. As I've said before, I'm not sure I'd have wanted to know the things that lay ahead. I like that I was so naïve and full of life and optimism. What is wrong with that? I might have made the connections between my bad experiences earlier and lost my hopeful attitude.

The younger Becky might have been incapable of seeing some connections between bad school experiences year after year, even when they were right in front of her. I know that all of the hurtful memories were inside of me, but I chose not to focus on them.

Was I afraid of becoming bitter? I knew I depended on people too much to resent them. One stereotype is that of the "bitter crip." I wanted to prove to the world that this was another assumption that needed shattering.

I saw my community as the friends who would always be there

for me. It was a self-selected group of people. Some of them would put things in perspective for me. My mother would always listen to what I was saying. She was a great person to bounce ideas off of.

I'm not sure that I would remove my disability if I could. The way I look at it, if I weren't disabled, I would be a completely different person. I think the outsider perspective is very important in a homogenizing society, and I take this role seriously.

Computers and Poetry
Dena

One night when Becky was close to graduating from UCSC, she and I sat talking with my brother John and my mother. Life was very good for Becky right then. It was her last quarter at the university; all her computer science classes were completed, and she decided to take a women's studies seminar. Becky told us she wasn't sure she'd fit in with the class because she wasn't a women's studies major. John began to list for her all the ways she *did* belong in the class—her writings on disability issues, her previous women's studies classes at a community college, her published article on being raised by a feminist mother, her public readings of some of these pieces—until Becky acknowledged, and was clearly pleased with, her qualifications for the class. Her interview the next day with the professor, Bettina Aptheker, went well, and she was admitted into the class.

Never before had Becky had such a class, one where she was fully appreciated and listened to. After every session she came home elated. Friends who knew Bettina told me she loved having Becky in her class, that she added so much to it.

This was a world of difference from Becky's computer science classes, where she clearly understood the subject but was under-recognized by her teachers. I'd overheard computer classmates say to her, "You really *know* that stuff!" And once someone told me, "My friend was in a class with Becky, and he said she's really smart, and that the teacher didn't treat her very well."

It's not surprising, then, that in her last few weeks at UCSC, Becky said to me, "I wonder if I made a mistake majoring in computer science?" We had a long discussion about how she could embark on another course of study if she wanted to, but computers were definitely a part of the future and would most likely be used in most fields, including women's studies. In fact, the reason Becky originally decided to study computer science was because she wanted to design programs for people with disabilities so they could have access to what wasn't available when she was young.

Ultimately, Becky said she did enjoy working with computers. It was just that she'd had such frustrating experiences in her classes. I noticed that she sent away for applications to several graduate schools in computer science, but she hasn't filled out even one.

Meanwhile, Becky was invited to read at *In Celebration of the Muse*, the annual poetry reading event for Santa Cruz women writers. She read a poem that she had written a couple of years earlier about her despair at what was happening at the university. Later, I heard many reactions from those who were there: some cried, some said they never understood what Becky had gone through, others said how courageous Becky was, and some were disappointed because they couldn't understand all her words. I felt it was a sharing with the community of what Becky's life is like. She stood on the stage in front of 300 people, nervous, stuttering, giving them a piece of herself. I was very, very proud of her.

The UCSC women's studies librarian, in attendance that night, sent Becky a letter asking if she'd like to work for the Women's Studies Department designing their website and doing other computer work. It was a temporary job, but Becky was very excited about it.

Recently, while an old friend of mine was visiting, Becky told her how some people talk to her in a loud or high voice, as if she were hard of hearing or a young child. A few days later this friend left a message on the answering machine, saying she couldn't stop thinking about what Becky had said, and asked if Becky would consider writing a poem about this and reading it while jazz musicians played behind her at a festival my friend was helping to organize in northern California. Becky called her back and said she'd never written a poem on demand before, but yes, she'd like to do it. The festival was scheduled for the weekend after graduation.

Some People
Becky

(read at Jazz by the Lake, *June 1996)*

I scare some people with my presence.
Not many know how to react when they see me.
There are strangers who use simple words
when talking to me.
Some raise the pitch of their voice.
Others increase the volume.

People I've never seen before
come up to tell me how lucky I am.
How brave.

People expect many things from me.
Some want me to teach them.
Some expect me to be stupid.
Others want me to solve
the world's problems.
Many are amazed that I'm just living my life.
Many don't listen to what I'm saying.
Many don't want to let go of their ideas.
However,
some
have.

One Sister Apiece
Becky

When we were growing up, I thought of Anna and myself as being outsiders. Because we changed schools so often, we were, so many times, the new kids in school. Also, our mother worked outside the home, while our father shopped and cooked. It seemed we had different values as well. I know Anna thought of us as outsiders, too. This had the effect of making us very close when we were young.

Change is a part of life, and all relationships go through changes. Sure enough, the ways I relate to Anna went through major changes. I'm not sure when we started to drift apart. I would like to think it was when she moved to Berkeley and I stayed in Santa Cruz. But recently, I found some of my early writings that indicated it may have started before that. The writing was about a long-standing communication problem where both of us were so wrapped up in our own point of view that neither could really hear what the other was saying.

We disagreed on whether or not I should go see my father for Feldenkrais sessions. Anna would insist that I continue the treatments with an open mind, even though the sessions would hurt, and I wasn't sure they were doing any good. "Maybe the reason you aren't seeing any results is because you don't believe it will work," she would tell me.

When I talk to Anna, my speech is clearer than when I speak to other people. Once, Anna interviewed me on tape for a performance she did for her senior project at Berkeley. On that tape, my speech was clearer than usual. That says something about the strength of our sisterly relationship.

Anna doesn't think of me as being all that disabled. She is younger than I, and grew up to accept me for who I am. Just as I, too, don't think of my cerebral palsy as being very severe. I am surprised when I hear anyone making a comment about the severity of my disability.

One person who makes these comments is our grandmother. I know that she has a very condescending attitude towards me. She thinks I can't do anything because of my "severe" disability. And, whenever I do anything right, she makes a very big deal about it. Quite rightfully this upsets Anna. Anna compares the treatment I receive to how my grandmother treats her. So, I understand why she has felt cheated. We have talked about our grandmother's attitude and Anna understands it isn't healthy for either one of us.

Now that we are both about to graduate from college, it is almost as if we aren't even taking in what the other is saying. I'm not sure when we began to not listen to each other. She is currently very critical of everything I am doing, including my decision to move back home and live with our mother.

My living independently has been a point of contention in recent years. It is Anna's view that I should always live on my own, at all costs. For a while, I shared her sentiment. I gave the roommate thing my best try for two years, but then decided it would be easier for me to move back with my mother while finishing school. Anna strongly disagrees with my decision. She even said, "I can't wait until you are living on your own again."

Her comment surprised me. I thought she, if anyone, would understand my previous problems, and see that this was only a temporary solution. She has had some not-so-great living arrangements herself. Anna is one of the people in my age group who can't understand how my mother and I could have a relationship based on being equals who live together.

Now that Anna is living in another city, I think whenever she sees our mother all of our mother's attention is focused on her. Anna probably thinks I have this sort of relationship with our mother, too. One night, she called up and complained to our mother that I was getting all of the attention.

When I call Anna these days, it is uncomfortable. We don't have much to say to each other. I am hoping that the universal law of change will take care of this. Until then, I will just have to wait out this form of sibling rivalry.

Graduations
Dena

Anna graduated from university first. She was 20 years old, and had received a full scholarship to UC Berkeley. The whole family went to see her senior project, which was a one-woman play she had written and would be performing. She borrowed a pair of Becky's old crutches to use as props, and sent me a copy of the play beforehand so I wouldn't be shocked. I was, a little.

As a child, Anna sometimes mimicked Becky's walk and mannerisms. One morning when I was in the kitchen making breakfast, Anna, three years old, crawled, not walked, into the kitchen. She pulled herself up on a chair, stood on tip-toes, arching her left foot the way Becky did, and laughed at her own antics. I laughed with her.

The first part of her senior project play was about a disabled girl, the middle was conversations between her and Becky, and the last part was about her own life. It was very good.

Becky graduated from UCSC a couple of years later, and again the whole family went to see her. But we didn't see her walk in, and couldn't see her on the stage with the other graduates, so her aunt Liz stormed backstage, demanding to know where Becky was. Liz came back to her seat and told us, sheepishly, they had arranged for Becky come onto the stage via a side door so she wouldn't have to do the walk and stairs. Becky was one of a very few women in that Computer Information Science graduating class, and the only disabled person. When they called her name, she received a big ovation.

Excerpt from Anna's Play

Anna: Becky, aren't you going to clean this up? Fine, I'll clean it up, and I'll finish doing the dishes for you too. My older sister, a year-and-a-half older. She has a stutter and she has spasms throughout her body.

Becky: When I'm standing up my knees are turned inward and so are my feet, a bit. And my right shoulder is higher than my left shoulder and my head is slightly over to the side. And my eyes used to be crossed but I had an eye operation and so they aren't anymore.

Anna: I was first told that my sister has cerebral palsy. She was born two-and-a-half months premature and her muscles weren't ready to walk, they told me. "But why aren't her muscles ready to walk now?" friends at school asked me.

Becky: I realized early on when I first began to look around at other people, I realized and I knew that I wouldn't be able to look like anyone else. And so I didn't try and so I didn't have to waste all that time trying to make my body look like something it wouldn't.

Anna: When the kids at school got older, they began to ask me is cerebral palsy "cerebral" and having to do with the mind or is it cerebral and having to do with the muscles?

Becky: Once I fell outside of the school cafeteria and people just started gathering all around me. And it was extremely humiliating because there I was, I mean, for me it just seemed like a simple fall and it was no problem for me to get up but people just started gathering from nowhere.

Anna: Her muscles are what's affected, cerebral. I could say now.

Becky: I really didn't like that and then they came over and started grabbing my arms, trying to help me up. I know they were well-meaning and everything.

Anna: When I moved away from home I realized I had extraordinary reflexes. I like to think I got them from catching Becky's falls.

Becky: My sister and I were both at the same school, and even though we had our different friends, we still would make sure and see each other during the day and eat.

Anna: An old pair of my sister's crutches. (Make noise with them.) These are a child's pair. These cuffs here are illegal, but Becky wanted cuffs that wouldn't allow her arms to slip out. But the crutches they make now come from France and are made out of fiberglass. They even come in different colors. Becky has a blue pair. My friends at school would always play in Becky's crutches as soon as she put them aside. But I never did.

Becky: To me my disability isn't all that important.

Anna: Becky, why don't you try going to Dad. He learned Feldenkrais work because you're his daughter. Why don't you let him work on you or at least try the exercises he has given you. Or just spend 5 minutes a day trying to relax. Don't you care about your body? Don't you want to be able to communicate to others easier?

Becky: I went to this women's solstice camp two summers in a row. The first summer I was 19 and there was this one person there and we'd do all these crazy things together and we'd stand up for each other and be young and goofy. And then the next year we got so lost we still laugh about that and we're still friends. I think part of that is because we're both on the outside of society and whenever we get together we always find something to laugh about no matter what it is.

Anna: Becky, remember when you and Mom and I took that trip to Oregon and Washington last summer? And Mom really wanted to take us to Crater Lake. But on the way we stopped at other extinct volcanos that had erupted thousands of years ago. And at one we hiked to the top of all that obsidian. And at the top we had a beautiful view of other extinct volcanoes, one filled with a lake.

The three of us hiked to the top; it was about a 45-minute hike, uphill. And everybody we passed on the trail was so amazed at you and encouraged you on. And Mom took close to a roll of film of you hiking. "Mom," I said, "just take a picture of the lake behind Becky, when we get to the top, you can say she swam across Oregon to get here."

Becky: To me it always felt like walking with rubber bands around your legs so that you couldn't straighten them and so that they hurt after you walked for a while.

Anna: I never knew I had the potential to walk fast until I moved away from home.

Becky: There was this one time I remember when me and some other people were thinking about planning a disability awareness day in my high school and I remember we thought of all these things that we could do to make people feel physically what it was actually like to live 24 hours a day with a disability.

My Trip to England
Becky

My father and his partner, Sue, had taken a short trip up to the part of Canada where he, my mother, my sister and I had lived when I was two years old. They had shown me the recent pictures, my father interspersing his memories from the past. He expressed an interest in going back and staying longer.

When I graduated from UCSC, he offered to take me on a trip to Canada. I thought this would be a good opportunity to bond with him by taking a road trip to a place which held significant associations for both of us, but one that I didn't remember at all. Also, it would be an interesting experiment to put the two of us together in a car for that amount of time.

Later, he told a group of his friends, in front of me, I had had the foolish idea to go up there. This was confusing to me, as I thought it was his plan for my graduation trip. I wish I could have found a way of expressing that thought to him.

But as it turned out, he had other ideas, so we settled on a four-week trip to Europe. I'm pretty sure he was thinking of this all along. We would spend the first two weeks in England. He is from England and I was born there but left at four months old.

A week and a half into the trip Sue was going to join us, then all three of us would visit other places in Europe together. But as I found out later, Sue's understanding was that it would be just the two of them after the first two weeks. My dad and I had talked about this possibility, but he bought my ticket for the whole four weeks.

My dad had had another family with two kids in England before us. Those children were almost exactly nine years older than my sister and me. They had visited us occasionally. I knew that my half-brother, Ben, was working as a computer programmer for the telephone company in London.

I heard stories through my growing-up years about a particular visit Ben made when I was only four years old. I remember bits and pieces from this time, but don't have any actual memories of him. He did another quick visit as a grown-up, but all I remember of that is seeing him for, maybe, half an hour.

When I realized I was going to go to England, my mother did a web search for my half-brother, and she and I started communicating with him. I told him about the upcoming trip, and he said he would like to see us when we came there. He gave me his phone number. I showed this email to my dad, who hadn't made contact with his son Ben for years.

On our first evening in London, my dad decided he wanted to go out for an Indian meal. After dinner, he told us what the bill was in pounds. He isn't usually a big tipper and he'll often ask me what 15% of the bill is. We got pounds and dollars mixed up, and he ended up leaving a 33% tip. The waiters were full of smiles and thanks for us when we left. It was as if they didn't know what to do with themselves.

A few days after we arrived, my dad decided it was time to contact Ben. He handed me the phone and said, "Since you've been in contact with him, you should be the one to call him." This was a surprise to me, but I did it. After the initial hellos, I handed the phone over to my dad. He arranged that we would meet at an Italian place that Ben knew about.

During dinner, Ben and I sat next to each other, and spent most of the time talking about computer programming. On the way back to where we were staying, my dad complained about the food at the restaurant. I said, "Dad, we just had a good meeting with your son and his wife, and all you can talk about is the food." Looking back, I wonder if he was jealous of me for having a connection with Ben.

A week after that, the plan was that we would go to

Cambridge, spend some time with my dad's sister and her husband, and then go on to Italy. (We weren't going to come back to London.) When we purchased our bus tickets though, the salesperson sold my dad round-trip tickets. I tried to say something to my dad, but he shushed me by saying, "You're making things unnecessarily confusing."

When we got to my aunt and uncle's house, Sue started complaining about me continuing on with her and my dad to the rest of Europe. She and Dad discussed finding me a bed-and-breakfast in Italy where I could stay while they went off on their romantic adventure. My aunt was sure I could stay with the family of a cousin in Italy whom I hadn't seen since I was three and didn't remember at all.

Neither of these suggestions appealed to me, and I called some of my mom's friends who lived in London who she knew from writing and publishing. I took the return bus ticket that my dad had bought, and one of my mom's friends went out of her way to pick me up on the other end, and made sure I got back to California safely.

Anna
Dena

I have a friend who projects a certain miserableness about her life, and she tells me my life is not so great either. She also thinks Anna's life has been changed by having Becky as a sister. I mention this to Anna when the two of us are in Mendocino celebrating her 23rd birthday.

"Changed? Of course my life's been changed," she says. "So what?"

"My acting coach says I lack a certain sense of security, or confidence." Anna tells me this as we are driving home. We have had a wonderful time together, and plan to do this more often. I don't see enough of her these days. "There's a boy in the class with a Down syndrome brother. The coach says the same thing to him. That he is insecure."

I think for a minute before saying anything. I know she has been hurt by all the attention given to Becky when they were growing up. Anna came out of the womb hearing praises for Becky's every accomplishment, while she, who grew up doing everything easily and well, was, I suppose, taken for granted. Even though, as a fast-running long-legged girl she heard her dad and me cheering at her soccer games. And, while Becky had weekly horseback riding lessons, Anna and I would hike together in the park or, if it was raining, hang out in the bookstore. And while Becky attended kindergarten at the Montessori school, Anna came with me to my Russian class at the community college. But nothing, apparently, made up for the focus on Becky.

I once asked Anna if she remembered the monster cookies we made for Becky to eat whenever she had thoughts of monsters. Anna was four then. "I sure do! I wasn't allowed to have even one!"

We have a picture on our wall of me squatting down to face a

seven-year-old Becky who's sitting
in my dad's chair at my parents'
house on Christmas Day. She is
feeling very bad because she has just
dropped and broken an elephant
cup that my brother gave Anna for
Christmas. Anna loves elephants. To
make things worse, it was the last
one in the store. In the picture, I am
trying to comfort Becky, who looks
absolutely miserable. I don't know
what I said, and I hope I gave Anna

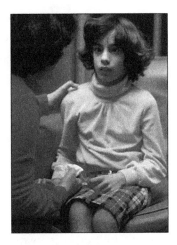

as much attention. After all, it was her cup. Since then, Becky has
been reluctant to hold someone else's valued things. I've seen her
shake her head no when people have held out fragile bowls or piles
of photographs they want kept in order.

As our car winds along the cliffs overlooking the Pacific
Ocean, I remember a dream Anna had when she was about seven.
"I got to this sort of adoption agency," she told me the morning
after the dream. "There I stayed for about a month. After a month,
everyone tried to call their mom and dad and go home. Well, most
of them went home and then it came my turn. I called and no one
answered. And then I called a second time and no one answered. I
just went home and knocked on the door and no one answered. I
went inside and I could hear you talking. I went into the living
room and there you were. Daddy was sitting in my seat and you
were over here and Becky was in the bathroom. You were talking
about making a thing for Becky in the bathroom. Then you looked
at me and then you just looked away and kept on talking like you
didn't even know me, like I was a stranger. Then I felt like no one
cared about me and I felt like going back."

I still remembered every word of the dream, which I had
written down at the time Anna told it to me.

She says to me now, while I'm driving, that the family doesn't care about her accomplishments, which include graduating with distinction from Berkeley at age 20.

"You think I don't care?" I ask her.

"Not you. I know you care."

"Who then?"

"The family."

It would be pointless to go through everyone, name by name. She feels, realistically or not, that what she does is not noticed.

"I know you feel the family doesn't care as much about you," I tell her, my voice unsteady. "But it's not true. Not true at all." She doesn't answer. Not a word. I take my eyes off the road and look at her. "Well you must know I don't feel that way. You are so very precious to me."

"I know that."

It may be that one of the things Anna loves about doing theater, which was her major in college, is that when she's on stage, all the people in the audience are paying attention to her. When she was about 11, I was invited to speak in front of a large group of women. I told her about it, and she blurted out, "You're so lucky!"

"Lucky?"

"Yes, all those women will be paying attention to you! You can say whatever you think is important and they'll be listening."

I thought this was rather a remarkable thing for a child to say. I took her comment seriously, and it helped me be less nervous about the speech. What I didn't realize then was how important this attention was to Anna.

We have talked a lot on this trip. In fact, whenever I am silent she asks me, "What are you thinking?" She wants to talk, or rather, wants me to talk.

"There are some good things about having a disabled person in the family," I say.

"Of course." she says, "Lots of things." We talk about the awareness, compassion, and sensitivity that we've developed, and how Becky has opened people's minds.

Having a disabled sister has made Anna extremely aware of others with disabilities, and she seems to know when and how to offer help. In fact Becky has had an impact on her entire extended family. Her six-year-old cousin amazed his teacher, who had cerebral palsy, with his sensitivity and understanding. And when Becky's uncle, who gives people driving tests for their license, took a young woman with cerebral palsy out for her test, he had a particular sensitivity, experience, and knowledge which few people in his position have.

Anna's life has of course been affected a great deal by having a sister with a disability. The negative parts must have included witnessing the teasing and the defending of Becky that Anna did at school. Anna never talked to me about this. What I did observe was that she often had to be the big sister, when in fact she is younger by twenty months. She was Becky's protector in many ways.

After changing her last name, at age eleven, to be different from Becky's, Anna must have felt some of the responsibility and attention on her as Becky's sister lift from her shoulders. When she entered junior high a year after Becky, no one, not the students or the teachers, knew her as the sister of Becky Taylor. After a few weeks, however, she told me that in class that day her math teacher said there was a girl in the seventh grade who could do complicated math problems in her head. Anna said she announced to the class: "That's my sister."

There were other times in their lives when Becky was the big sister. Any time Anna needed help with math, Becky had the answer. And because she saw that Becky successfully left high school after the 10th grade and went to a community college, Anna had the courage to do it too.

On Becky's twentieth birthday, I had to fight back the tears as Anna told her how important she was in her life, how much she had learned from her, how much she appreciates Becky. And I am very touched when I look through the stack of homemade birthday cards I've saved that Anna made for Becky over the years.

Earlier that day as Anna and I sat on the bluffs overlooking the ocean at Gualala, she asked if I was worried about her. No, I'm not, I told her, but I know that she gets stressed out, and that concerns me. She is working full time and looking for another part-time job so she can afford more acting classes.

"Do you think I'm getting too involved with my acting?" she asks me.

My mind spins fast, wondering what she is really asking, but I say, "If it's what you want to do, if it's your passion, then I think it's wonderful that you're doing it."

I have no doubt that she can juggle all these things in her life, including a boyfriend and long bicycle trips on the weekends. Anna is the most organized person I know. When she was two years old she would set out the clothes for her and Becky to wear the next day—shoes and socks, with pants, t-shirts, and underwear neatly folded on top—according to what she thought the weather would be.

And that's how I always think of Anna: completely responsible, mature beyond her years, capable of everything. She is immensely observant, listens to everything going on, takes it all in, asks questions, remembers it all. We always asked Anna where things were when we lost them, and she always knew. Becky, on the other hand, if she couldn't find her shoes, would sit on the floor in her room saying, "shoes, shoes," and someone, usually Anna, would find them for her.

On the last night of our trip, we have a drink in the old Gualala Hotel before going up to our room. We smile at each other. "It's funny we're not talking," she says.

Dual Realities
Becky

After I received my B.A. in Computer Science, I joined some computer-related job search email lists. I was living at home at the time. These were lists that sent out job announcements to people who were interested. Many of the jobs listed required years of experience in programming languages that I hadn't studied in school. I did apply for those jobs I felt qualified for, and developed a file folder of rejection letters. The majority of jobs for people just out of college without real-world experience were in customer service. I knew that my stutter would make a telephone job impossible.

Meanwhile, my mother had started a new position at her work and was going to meetings with people from employment agencies and coming home saying, "People with your skills can write their own ticket. Computer Science people are in so much demand." When I asked where to apply, she didn't know, and this made me feel even lower for not being able to find a job.

I applied for one position through a headhunter in San Francisco. I took public transportation (bus, bus, bus, train, bus) to get to his office. It took four hours. I thought this headhunter might be an "in," even if this job didn't work out. When the headhunter saw me coming into his office, he said, "The interview has been cancelled." I asked him to please keep me in mind for any future openings. He said he would. I left and didn't get any job offers from him again.

She's 27 Now
Dena

I've stopped telling her to be careful,
to watch for slippery leaves and potholes,
cars and carpet edges.

I've stopped telling her to relax
so her words
will come out easier.

I've nearly stopped telling her
not to chew with her mouth open.
She doesn't do it that much
anymore anyway.

I'm going to stop telling her
to consider graduate school
where she'd be among peers
who might appreciate her thinking.

Yes, mothernagging is stopping right now.
It is time.
She is an adult.

That Voice
Becky

I start hearing it even before I'm up again.
This insistence and demand.
Even before I've hit the ground,
or realize what I've hurt.

If I were superstitious, I might
think of it as a blessing or a curse
to have my mother's voice in my head.
I am more careful because of it.

I didn't use to look for clues in every fall.
Why did this happen?
What can I do to prevent it in the future?
These questions have free reign of my brain.

Falling is commonplace for me.
There are times when I fling my crutches away from me.
Sometimes, people gather around to see if they can help.
They used to grab my armpits and pull me up.
This doesn't work so well.
It is hard to instantaneously regain my balance.
It is best if I get up on my own.
Sometimes, I let someone pick up my crutches.

I am embarrassed by my falls.
They're an indication that
I did something wrong. This isn't good.
Falls are always going to be there.
One day, I'll find my balance.

Dialing 9 from the Moon
Becky

I'm here! I made it to my dream. I wanted to work for a start-up company, and now I do. I like the feeling that we are all working for a common goal. This web-based e-commerce company has products, news and information for and about people with disabilities. The company goal is amazing to me after years of feeling alone with my disability. This is the company that I thought I wouldn't find, the job that is too good to be true.

Everything is slightly different, though. I somehow envisioned long nights of problem solving over and after dinner. Instead of putting our heads together, we have separate offices or cubicles. We email or call each other, hoping that our questions are answered. We go into someone else's office only if we see that the person isn't busy. I'm unsure of where I belong or what I'm supposed to be doing.

I go in early and get home late, and I'm tired. My life has become solely focused around this job. The only meaningful social interactions I have are with the other people at work. On two out of the four weekends on this job so far, I have worked both days. One weekend I was supposed to crop and prepare 500 images for the website. Urgent requests for tasks came to me from people in several departments. I prepared the newsletter and maintained the website for the company.

There is nothing cozy or neighborly about what I've found in Sunnyvale. The restaurant closest to my work has branches all over. Even the "corner health-food store" is a chain. The first poster that I saw on the Community Bulletin Board was for a Fly-In, fifty miles away in Santa Cruz County. Isn't there anything closer? The weekly paper has Santa Cruz ads.

I do miss being a local and feeling like I belong somewhere, but would I fit in anymore? I'm living in a hotel now. When my grandmother came to visit once, she noticed there was no one outside, even in the day. "This is like the moon," she told me. I felt the same way; it was a strange place. There weren't even any windows in my room that would open. I called home every night for some reassurance. I'm not sure I recognize or even like the person I've become. I feel the job has changed me in ways I don't quite understand.

My job and I move to Mountain View after a few months. Then a year later, the company does what so many other dot-com companies do at that time, and closes altogether. I stay and look for another job for a while. My friends finally convince me to move to the San Francisco Bay Area because, they say, it is a good place for people with disabilities.

Rejecting Stem Cell Treatment
Becky

In 2009, a friend of ours emailed my mother to say that she was looking into stem cell therapy for her own illness, and thought it might help me. She sent the website of a place that did stem cell treatment in the Dominican Republic. We looked into it and even arranged a phone conversation with the doctor (of psychology) in charge. First he spoke to my mother and he told her to send $30,000 and bring me in for treatment. When he talked to me, he answered my questions and then he told me that I wasn't a good candidate for his clinic.

I still wonder if he said that because he could tell I wasn't at death's door, so to speak, and therefore wouldn't be a good advertisement for him, or because he sensed I was skeptical of his clinic. Either way, the implication was off-putting.

We did a lot of web research on this place, and, as with everything else online, there were people who thought his stem cell clinic was overblown and overrated and others proclaiming it to be the best thing to come along. In the end, we decided there were too many fishy things about that clinic. So, we gave up and looked elsewhere.

We found another clinic in Germany. (There were none in the United States.) It had an online questionnaire that I reluctantly filled out, and I got accepted pending an MRI. My doctor, having strong doubts about stem cell treatment, refused to authorize the MRI. His refusal took me on a parallel path of muscle relaxants, and physical and speech therapy. I had my doubts about going to Germany anyway. This clinic would have used my own cells, called adult stem cells. The cells would be taken from my hip, altered in some way (we never could find out what was done), and days later, they would inject these cells into a different part of my body.

One of the things that became blatantly apparent from our research was that anything and everything can help somebody. I think this holds true for all forms of bodywork, but is highlighted more when dealing with something that is indescribable and/or new. The stem cell clinic websites were full of stories from people who had tried everything else for their kids and nothing had worked before stem cell treatments. We wondered, though, how many of the positive outcomes were due to the placebo effect.

We realized that many of the featured stem cell patients were young children, and most reported having to go back multiple times. Also, we found accounts of negative effects from the treatments. I wasn't willing to subject myself to something that could be dangerous for an unspecified outcome.

A central premise of the current understanding and research on stem cells seems to be that the body is supposed to know where the damage is and direct these new cells to that place. I can imagine this for an illness, accident or stroke victim, but my body has only (and always) known cerebral palsy.

When we looked online, we found lots of criticism and discussion about the ethics of how the fetal stem cells were gathered, but none about how the patients were preyed upon. I didn't like the way these clinics promised us the contact information of previous patients, but wouldn't give that to us until after we paid. It seemed these places were more interested in getting our money and getting us to their clinics than in examining potential patients to see whether they thought the treatment would work.

At some point in our search, my mother emailed a stem cell researcher at Stanford who said that since I was functioning well and happy with my life, she wouldn't recommend stem cell therapy at this experimental stage. Eventually, we came to agree with her.

CPA by 40?
Becky

Most years around my birthday, I like to take a look at my life and see where I'm going. I ask myself what I want to change and where I want to be in a year.

After my computer job fell apart in 2001, I spent a year and a half in the San Francisco Bay Area looking for work and found myself in a depressing housing situation. So I moved back to Santa Cruz to live with some friends my own age. I also went back to the Department of Rehabilitation and attended a job search group. There was a gathering of women computer professionals at which the speaker told us that it was perfectly okay to be a barista at Starbucks. Then a job developer told me that I can't do well in interviews and I should take a $3,000 course in grant writing her friend was teaching in San Jose, 45 miles away, that I would have to pay for myself. After these experiences, I decided to go back to Cabrillo College and study accounting.

In my second accounting class, I found out that in order to become an accountant, one had to do a certain number of hours of work under a certified accountant. This idea of working under a professional really appealed to my sensibilities at the time. What if that had happened when I got my B.A. degree in Computer Information Sciences some years ago? This would have provided me with real-world experience and connections that might have helped me find a job after graduation. At the end of my Quick-Books class, the instructor said that she sometimes hears about new job openings, and any of her students could email her and get those job listings. This is how I got my first bookkeeping position even before getting my accounting degree. Also, accounting, unlike computer programming, was more of a female field of study. This made me feel less like it was an uphill struggle. I think, if I had it to do over again, I would go into accounting instead of computer science.

I got my accounting degree at age 33. The following spring semester I started a student-worker job at Cabrillo in a fiscal capacity. As a student worker, I had to be continually enrolled in at least six units (usually two classes) to keep the job.

After a year, I switched from doing fiscal support to doing complex computer spreadsheets and other computer problem-solving tasks for one of the deans. This dean had been my second computer science instructor when I was 17 and new to Cabrillo. He wanted his staff to attend some of Cabrillo's planning meetings, and at one of these meetings I found out that because of budget problems, Cabrillo was threatening to eliminate all student-worker positions and also cut the class offerings that weren't necessary for a degree.

All of this led me, at 35, to decide that I wanted to become a Certified Public Accountant by age 40. I talked to a transfer counselor who looked at my records and told me that I would have to take two economics classes if I wanted to transfer. When it was time for me to register for the next semester, I saw that those two classes were offered one right after the other in the same room with the same teacher two mornings a week. This is perfect, I thought.

I enjoyed my economics classes, and when I was getting ready for classes and work that semester, knowing I once again had a goal, I would smile at my reflection in the mirror. It was a small thing, but it created a positive loop in my mind. Seeing my smiling face made me feel better about myself. Although both of my front top teeth were discolored from a fall that had necessitated a root canal, I didn't see that at the time.

The finances of the college improved slightly, or at least I stopped hearing how they were going to cut all the student jobs. I stayed at my student-worker job for three more years. One day I figured out that I had been in school for thirty years of my life. This realization depressed me. After a series of bad falls that knocked out one of my front teeth and loosened the other one, I finally decided it wasn't worth it anymore for me to continue. The stress of having to carry six units while working was getting to me, and I was no longer interested or excited about learning. In my burned-out mode I would take classes that I thought would be the easiest.

Finding Crumbs
Dena

When you were seven
and said we should enjoy
every crumb of every minute
of every day,

you didn't know
there would be minutes, days
too terrible to enjoy
too dark to find even crumbs

But still
somehow
that young spirit
endures

WILD
Becky

After UCSC, I became curious about disability activism groups, and have since taken comfort and pride in being a member of such organizations.

My first involvement was to join an email list for people with cerebral palsy; it also included parents of kids with CP and people training to be special education teachers. We were all asking and answering questions of each other. At that time it filled a need inside of me to be a part of a global community. When I moved to Sunnyvale, the volume of emails got to be too much, and I removed myself from the discussion.

At one point a housemate knew of an opening on a local disability access committee. I joined that group until I moved to a different city in the county and was no longer eligible to be a member. This group, however, gave me a taste for what disability groups could accomplish.

After I left my job at Cabrillo, I started hanging out with some of my friends who have done a lot for the Santa Cruz disability community. I would go with them to the bus company's board of directors meetings and speak my mind. These friends lived at the St. George, an historic old hotel in Santa Cruz that had been converted into studio apartments. It soon became clear to me that I didn't want to continue in my current living situation. So, I asked one of my friends if she thought I could get a place at the St. George. Eventually, I did.

At the time, these friends were on the Santa Cruz County Commission on Disabilities. I attended meetings and participated as much as possible from the sidelines. When the opportunity arose to join a sub-committee of the Commission, I signed up.

After our first few meetings, it became clear to everyone

involved that we were more than a sub-committee and needed to form our own group. Some of us knew other people who we wanted to invite. We renamed the group Women Independently Living with Disabilities (WILD).

WILD has gotten some of our members to be on the Commission on Disabilities. Now, the majority of the Commission members are also in WILD and, starting last year, for the first time in its history, the Commission chairperson and vice-chair are both women. That is the power of WILD. When the people at an assisted living facility in the area came to the Commission asking for help getting bus service restored to their area, it was the WILD members who went to the bus company's meeting and spoke about how hard it is for some of us to get around. WILD members come from all over the county and have differing interests. We meet for lunch, talk about issues, and support each other in different ways when it is appropriate.

I am now not only a member of WILD, but also the vice chair of the Santa Cruz County Commission on Disabilities. It was one of these WILD members who invited me to join her on the In-Home Support Services Advisory Committee and someone else who told me that I was needed on the Metro Advisory Committee. It brings me joy to know there are such organizations exploring issues of importance and helping people with disabilities.

Epilogue
Dena

Becky's life has not turned out as I thought it would. I imagined an easier life. This was a girl with an amazing mathematical and logical mind, and an indomitable spirit to go with it. As an infant she lay in bed one night saying "Grows, dies, grows, dies…" "What are you talking about?" we asked. "Life," she answered. As a seven-year-old she put on Anna's roller skates and told me she was going to try them out. "Really?" I asked. "Yes. You can either come outside and watch me, or you can stay in here."

I thought people, companies, organizations, colleges would want her on their team just to *think*. But no. She is disabled. She walks and talks funny. This makes people uneasy. And it makes me mad, and sad, and wondering if there's anything I can do to change this, and then asking myself if I should relax, breathe, and understand that Becky is happy and is changing the world in small, important ways.

Becky now lives in a place she loves in downtown Santa Cruz. She is near a terrific bookstore, several good restaurants, movie theaters, stores, and a great museum. She does freelance computer work, is active in disability organizations, takes care of her body, and has friends and family who love her. She is fiercely independent, and has a wonderful sense of humor. You would be lucky to know her.

Resources

Cerebral palsy (CP) is an umbrella term that refers to a group of disorders affecting a person's ability to move. It is a permanent life-long condition, but generally does not worsen over time. It is due to damage to the developing brain either during pregnancy or shortly after birth (from www.cerebralpalsy.org.au). See also www.cerebralpalsy.org, and ucp.org, the official website of United Cerebral Palsy.

Disability.gov. The U.S. federal government website has information on disability programs and services nationwide. The site connects people with disabilities, their families and caregivers to helpful resources on topics such as how to apply for disability benefits, find a job, get health care or pay for accessible housing. You can also find organizations in your community to help you get the support you need. Site has information for people with disabilities, teachers, (e.g., accommodations and support in the classroom and IEPs), parents, employers and others.

Feldenkrais Method. This gentle method of movement education improves posture, strength, flexibility, range of motion, and coordination. It eases painful, protective ways of moving, minimizes physical, physiological, and psychological stress, nurtures self-expression, enhances self-image, and makes moving a joy. See www.Feldenkrais.com and www.MindinMotion-online.com.

Many Names Press. See www.ManyNamesPress.com (Kate Hitt) for links to the *Tell Me the Number before Infinity* facebook pages, website and blog to see discussions about this book.

Parent support. There are many online resources. Here are three:

Center for Parent Information and Resources. Connects parents with groups and resources in their area. Also included are resources for educators. (www.ParentCenterhub.org)

Children's Disabilities Information. An annotated list of support groups and listservs for parents of children with disabilities or special needs. (www.ChildrensDisabilities.info)

Friendship Circle. Resources, groups, information. (www.FriendshipCircle.org)

Sibling support. (https://www.SiblingSupport.org). Sibnet is an online community of support and information for adult brothers and sisters of disabled siblings. See their paper *What Siblings Would Like Parents and Service Providers to Know*. Site also has information and support for younger siblings.

Teacher support. www.Lesley.edu/special-education-resources, disability.gov, www.ParentCenterHub.org, & www.4Teachers.org

Therapeutic Horseback Riding. This uses the sport of horseback riding to encourage children, teens and adults with special challenges in many areas: physical skills (strength, coordination, balance), cognitive functioning (memory, cause and effect, perception), emotional well-being (self-esteem, confidence), social skills (sharing, following directions, social cues, patience), and education knowledge (vocabulary, colors, shapes and numbers). See www.AmericanHippoTherapyAssociation.org

Colophon

Many Names Press
believes in the power of published literature
to overcome injustice and warring minds,
to develop work parity & equality,
to foster respect for women & children everywhere,
to support, nurture & protect this world
for all beings.

Adobe's Robert Slimbach designed this postscript text type *Minion* in 1989. Its shape is based on hot type created by Nicolas Jenson in Mainz in 1470, Venetian printer & publisher Aldus Manutius and his punch-cutter, Francesco Griffo in 1501, and the Parisian Claude Garamond in 1545. *Minion* has a legible and pleasant appeal, and is well suited for printing poetry because of its clean feet, well proportioned small caps and text figures.

MANY NAMES PRESS
KATE HITT
POST OFFICE BOX 1038
CAPITOLA, CALIFORNIA USA
95010-1038